GOD OF THE GRAY AREAS

GOD OF THE GRAY AREAS

learning to see the
light of heaven
in everyday life

JENNIFER LOPES

WHP
Wyatt House Publishing

Mobile, Alabama
www.wyattpublishing.com

Wyatt House books may be ordered through
booksellers or by contacting:
WYATT HOUSE PUBLISHING
399 Lakeview Dr. W.
Mobile, Alabama 36695
www.wyattpublishing.com
editor@wyattpublishing.com

*Because of the dynamic nature of the Internet, any web address or links
contained in this book may have changed since publication and may
no longer be valid. The views expressed in this book are solely those of
the author and do not necessarily reflect those of the publisher, and the
publisher hereby disclaims any responsibility for them.*

Cover design by: Mark Wyatt
Author photo courtesy of: Michele West
Stylist and makeup for author photo:
Phrankey Lowery and Jessica Price

ISBN 13 TP: 978-0-9882209-9-7
Library of Congress Control Number: 2013939711

Printed in the United States of America

GOD OF THE GRAY AREAS

"If ever there was a woman after God's own heart, it is Jennifer Lopes. She has grown to be a powerful force for Jesus in our generation. She inspires me, from her gift of sign language interpretation, to her daily fight for the unborn. Jennifer reaches out to the hearts of desperate pregnant women who need guidance.

I have personally cried out in the darkest hours of my own life and I witnessed God use Jennifer's words to speak peace back into my life. I have always said that Jennifer has raised two of the most beautiful, Jesus-filled children I have ever seen, and that speaks greatly about her character. Jennifer is the real deal with a message of God's infinite favor in her personal life. "As he is, so are we in this world" is evident in Jennifer's life because she has this same spirit. She is a visionary and leader in the Kindgom. She leads people to the cross. She is a legacy-leaver. I'm the first to recommend her book. It goes great with my morning coffee."

-*Deidre Pujols*
Wife of Los Angeles Angels first baseman, Albert Pujols
President of Pujols Family Foundation
CEO of Pujols Kitchen, LLC

"Jennifer Lopes has a heart for the sanctity of human life that is second to none in my circle of acquaintances. She has the ability to deliver a message of forgiveness, love and compassion with a nonstop passion for our youth and young adults. This message is so needed for the future of the church. In a time where our culture is creating an environment of no consequence, *God of the Gray Areas* brings a message of Purity, Truth and Justice."

Doug Holtzmann
Conference Director, Joyce Meyer Ministries
St. Louis, MO

"Jennifer has been the strongest Christian influence over my life through the example of her endless service and love for Christ. I can clearly see the Holy Spirit shining through her ministry. This book gives you a glimpse into Jennifer's heart as she uses her own life experiences to beautifully illustrate how scripture can be applied to any circumstance in life. I hope that all who read her book will be inspired and blessed in their walk with Jesus the same way her words have impacted me."

Kimberly Crossett
Vice President, Athlete Marketing
Los Angeles, California

DEDICATION

This book is dedicated to my family: my husband, Hugh- the love of my life- and my children, Naomi and Caleb.

Hugh, your constant example of diligence and steadfast love for our Lord has inspired me over the years. You are a wonderful father and husband. Thank you for your support, prayers and encouragement to follow the call of God for my life. I still request that I be married to you in Heaven.

Caleb and Naomi, I am so proud to be your mom and count it a holy privilege. The way God has blessed you makes me stand in awe. I will forever thank Him that He chose and allowed me to be in your family. Never compromise the truth and if you do, repent quickly, get up, and take a giant step forward. Always.

I want to thank my mom and dad for their love over the years. Mom, thank you for always asking when the book was going to be ready and teaching me to believe God as a child. Dad, thank you for being my biggest fan. I know of no one who brags on their daughter as much as you do. You taught me how to be proud of my children. I inherited bragging rights from you - for sure.

I want to thank my spiritual mom, Joyce Meyer, for her relentless display of courage and strength. Even from afar, through her books and teachings, she has taught me how to be a strong woman in ministry and to live with excellence and love as my goal.

CONTENTS

INTRODUCTION
A PRAYER FOR YOU

As I was praying, the Lord reminded me of the horrible pit from which He rescued me. He reminded me that in my current failures that I am not disqualified to proclaim His goodness. As Paul said, I have been the chief of sinners, so shall I also admit. Like Paul I also now can say that I bear the scars of serving Christ in my body.

This prompted my prayer for each of you:

If the attack that has come against your life can stand up to a Holy God, then let it remain. If the ones who seek your demise can stand up to your Holy God, then let them stand. If the trouble that you face is stronger than the blood of Jesus, then let it stand. If the sickness in your body is more powerful than the stripes of Jesus, then may it continue. If the lies of the enemy are more full of truth than God's Word, then may

11

they not be removed. If your sins cannot be washed by the blood of Jesus then may they never be blotted out. If your oppressors continue to shake their fists at God and are triumphant then may they take their crowns and trophies. However....

If the God you serve, if the Word He is, and if the healing and truth in Him are YOURS then may every bondage, every stronghold, every disease, every lie, and every attack wither and die from it's very root. May the trees of wickedness bear fruit no more in your life and in your present circumstances.

I wish to declare over you that your imperfections cannot stand in front of a Holy God. Your trust in Jesus has made and will make your weaknesses now perfected in Him. He is your Advocate. He is your Healer. He is your Truth. Nothing that wishes to accuse you can stand against this Holy God. He is for you - not against you. He is greater in you than he (the devil) that is in the world.

If you are in Christ - may your sins look for you and find you not. May your disease search you out and find you not. May your enemies ravage the earth over and find you not. For you are hidden in Christ. Can they find you? You are in the tower of His name. When the darkness seeks for you and finds you not... may you and your Lord laugh. For He is the God who laughs at the wicked.

Amen.

WHAT'S IN A NAME

Ever heard of Prissy Hawkins? Silver Starky? Or Starla Goff? Well, in case you haven't met them...let me introduce you. Prissy is a real estate agent whom I have never met. I read her name on a real estate sign in the city where I currently live. I was tempted to be jealous of her because her mom gave her such an interesting name. Silver is a few years older than me and attended my high school. And Starla, well, she is a fellow baseball mom and I will tell you why I stole her identity.

I used to have a boring name. It was boring until J-Lo became famous and then my name was fun - for a while. I became Jennifer Lopes before the other one became well known so I have somewhat grown into the famous name. I still long for a more interesting title and couldn't resist my urge to start changing it on occasion. The first time it happened was at a conference in Columbus, Ohio. My friend and I went for Starbucks. When they took my order and asked my name to write on the cup... it rolled off of my tongue like southern, homegrown honey. "Staaaaarla," I said. With no hesitation my friend shot me a glance as if I had beamed an imaginary pole into the room. She was visibly uncomfortable as the fellow asked me, "How do you spell that?" "S - T - A - R - L - A," I said with a wink. Keep in mind we were attending a Christian Conference and she was the Conference Director - for Joyce Meyer Ministries.

She got so embarrassed by my secret lie that she almost forgot her own name while she ordered her coffee. She grabbed my arm and said, "Why did you lie?" I told her how I just wanted to see what it was like to have such an authentic name and that from now own my official Starbucks name would be......(drum roll please)..........'Staaaaarla." She said that she would pray for me as she tried to cover her grin. I have tried that trick on a few friends since then and it makes each of them wiggle with outward discomfort. But lately I have been thinking of switching it up by using "Silver" or "Prissy." Maybe I will try something more Trump-ish like "Ivanca." Who knows?

It's apparent that I have a fondness for people's names and always like to tell them the meanings and origins of them. I am especially interested in the names of the Bible and am intrigued by God's purposeful changing of them. He seemed to inform people of their new names just when they were up for a major life change or stepping into their destiny. As we know, Saul, became Paul. Sarai, was renamed Sarah. Abram, became Abraham. Remember Jacob, the worm? He was transformed into Israel. What a name! I started to name my Caleb - Caleb Israel, and I talked myself out of it. What was I thinking?

Better yet, God may have a new name for Caleb. I just wonder what it will be. I wonder what yours will be. I have mentioned that Adam had the task of naming the animals. Why would God ask him to do that? Apparently, names are important to our Father, too. God has a Kingdom name in store for each of us. Ask Him what it is. He may tell you. Until that time, make sure that you are answering to what the Word of God says about you and not what the world tells you. We can live up to the names we have been given - Children of God. This doesn't mean that we will be perfect. It just means that we have a Daddy who places a name of "Redeemed" over us and that He will never leave us or forsake us.

So, if you bump into me at the coffee shop and overhear me spelling out "Charro," lighten up. It's all just for fun. It's a gray area.

THE FIELD OF ICE CREAM DREAMS

To save her from any infamy I will simply call her Ms. K. I learned of her devout love for ice cream as we sat next to each other at a rather boring baseball game. She went on and on about her favorite ice cream and how she had stopped at five places on the drive to the field and had no luck getting her hands on the dessert. She mentioned how two places had broken machines and the other places were simply out of ice cream altogether. She just wasn't letting her craving wane. The conversation seemed to be incessant about the flavors, textures and was overplayed; much like our ball team.

Inside I asked myself, "Five stops?" She is a persistent type; I knew I liked her. So, as is common for me, and in my arrogance I said aloud, "I think that after stop number two you should have just accepted that God was showing you that it was not in 'the afternoon plans' for you to have ice cream." No one thought another thing about it until...

The sneak attack and a covert operation showed up. All of heaven was fully engaged to show us mere humans that we don't know it all. At that very moment I saw out of the corner of my eye and only three feet from the bleachers - a sight that I will never forget. Without notice the ICE CREAM MAN rolled up to us in his colorful truck.

I pointed, "Look! Look! Ms. K, the Lord must really love you!" She erupted into screams. I erupted into screams. Everyone thought that we were cheering for the ball team but no play was happening. Before we knew it everyone rushed the truck to celebrate.

It was a lesson learned for me. Number one - delay does not mean denial when it comes to God's blessings. How much more did Ms. K see God following her down the street? Number two - I was reminded that if He will do that for her that I am in line for the same kind of treatment. Number three - I will be more careful to say what I think are God's plans. He is able to show me up at any given time.

Once I got home I settled onto my sofa with an ice

cream cream cone with the family. We toasted to the goodness of God that afternoon with our own pop-sicles. Then it suddenly occurred to me that the ice cream man was such a kind guy. He said "God bless you" to each one who purchased a cone. God spoke to my heart. He reminded me that this gentle soul was trying to make a living and needed the money in a bad way. He whispered, "Jen, I would cause every machine in that city to break down if it took getting Mr. Ice Cream Man an answered prayer." I silently thanked God for supplying Ms. K and Mr. Ice Cream's needs all at the same time.

I now have an insatiable craving like Ms. K. Not only do I desire a couple of gallons of ice cream but I long to savor it with my Savior, who is able to do exceed-ingly... abundantly... above... all that we can ask or think.

Our "thinking" can never figure out the Mysteries of God. It's not a gray area, that God wants to give us the desire of our hearts.

Spam - The Food of Angels

I approached the front of the church and felt something strange. Maybe it was because it was a weekday and it felt so vacant – so empty...until I spotted the scared looking seeing- eye dog near the door. I have never seen a seeing- eye dog that looked scared before so I decided to avoid it. I made a sharp left turn to find another entrance. There, to my left, was a tiny woman seated on the flowerbed retainer wall. She had a head covering, dark glasses, and oversized handbag.

I asked her how she was and really didn't want it to be more than a rhetorical question. She said, 'I am still alive so I am good – I guess." I immediately went to her and fell on my knees in front of her. It didn't take me long to discover that her dog was much less fearful than her. She was a wreck. She began to tell me that she had been in an accident three months ago that blinded her. She was stranded and was also pregnant, hungry and scared.

I offered prayers for her and from my right emerged her husband with brown bag in hand. I introduced myself and asked what else I could do. I opened his bag and saw several cans of Spam, a phone book, and a crisis pregnancy brochure. The need seemed so great. I kept glancing back at this blind woman's dirty coat. They had spent the night outdoors. They both were intelligent, sober and God-seeking people. I did what any person with a heart would do. I gave them a lift to McDonalds. But I left them there. What else could I do? I am still asking myself that question.

Later that day, as I drove to pick up my weekly delivery of coupons I saw this couple walking, with brown bag in hand, near the church. This time I didn't stop. What else could I say? What else could I do?

Over dinner that night I recounted the day's events to my family. My children had the answer. I have come to find that kids haven't had fear ingrained in them like us. My son Caleb said, "We have it too good. They are supposed to be here, now, having dinner with us, Mom." I felt the weepiness come over me that I have come to embrace. He pressed further. "Mom, people are dying out there and we are sitting here worried about being 20 minutes late to school. We are spoiled rotten." Hebrews 13:2 says, *Do not forget to entertain strangers, for by so doing some people have entertained angels without knowing it.*

We are blessed. We can make a difference. God told us to take strangers into our homes but conventional wisdom says, no. "Then He also said to him who invited Him, 'When you give a dinner or a supper, do not ask your friends, your brothers, your relatives, nor your rich neighbors, lest they also invite you back, and you be repaid. But when you give a feast, invite the poor, the maimed, the lame, the blind. And you will be blessed, because they cannot repay you; for you shall be repaid at the resurrection of the just." Luke 14:12-14.

This is a challenge for me and for you. I dare say that some of us wouldn't even feed our dog Spam. Let's ask God to show us what we can do for the hurting, the lost, and the desperate.

I hope that you entertain angels, unaware. Pray I can have that courage too, so the light of Heaven pushes away the darkness around us.

DANCING WITH THE STARS

There we were during the height of the praise and worship service at a long-awaited and much anticipated meeting. The music was hopping and so were a few people – literally. This one man, in particular, was dancing in a way that would put King David to shame. He seemed a pro at worship and had no reservations. I have seen this man many times over the years. He is known to cross a stage, wave a flag, or dance over the pews. He's the Christian version of Dancing with the Stars; he just has an invisible partner.

Now this is where it gets interesting. As soon as the worship was over and it was time for the message something tragic happened. Let me break it down for you. Dude-dancer fell fast asleep.

I couldn't stop staring at him. I looked to see if I had any breathe-right strips in my purse because he was hard at it. Snoring. During. The. Preaching. The audacity! The shamelessness!

I looked around to see if anyone was looking at him. Then, apologetically, I looked to see if anyone was looking at me – looking at him. I sat there amazed. I began to think of all the reasons that he had fallen asleep. Maybe he was sick. Maybe he was in deep prayer and dozed off. Maybe he had sleep apnea. Bingo! That had to be the answer.

As soon as I found my conclusions I felt that familiar feeling that Father God was peeking over my shoulder. Without hesitation, I knew He would be asking me why I had become an investigative reporter slash-medical student all of a sudden.

The Lord, in His loving manner, reminded me that I should be paying attention to my own sleeping disorder. My disorder is spiritual in nature. I would never be caught napping in the middle of a service because my pride is too lofty. I am not any different than the Dude-Dancer.

Sleeping in the natural is better than to be snoozing regarding God's will toward situations in my life. The Bible says in Ephesians 5:14-17 "Awake, O sleeper, and arise from the dead, and Christ will shine on you. Look carefully then how you walk, not as unwise but as wise, making the best use of the time, because the days are evil. Therefore do not be foolish but understand what the will of the Lord is."

I pray that you and I both will arise from our sleep and awaken to the will of God for our lives.

Spookfish

Spookfish. Sounds like something out of a science fiction novel. Not so. I read about them in an interesting excerpt from the latest Smithsonian Institute magazine. Let me share: "The rarely seen spookfish dwells in dark ocean depths, where bioluminescent flashes from other creatures can be the only light. When scientists this past year caught a live spookfish for the first time in the South Pacific, they found it had two elaborate eyes that are positioned to capture light from both above and below. Stranger still, reflective crystals focus light onto the retina-making the spook fish the only vertebrate whose vision is based on mirrors."

As studious as I was being by reading the latest scientific findings I couldn't help but have flashbacks of the movie Finding Nemo. Do you remember Dory, the blue tang fish, that Nemo's Dad befriended while searching for Nemo? Of course you do. I may have been reading this article while sitting on my front porch but in my mind I dove there- to the deepest part of the ocean - reliving the moment when Dory got lost exactly where the Smithsonian was talking about. My question became this. If the spookfish has just now been discovered this past year, according to scientists, how in the world did Dory confront that "spooky fish" that was described like the one the scientists report? You may recall that spooky fish that flashed bioluminescent currents of what looked like electrical charges. It even had the funny eyes that were drawn toward movements of whatever happened to come near it. It seemed clear to me that the writers and illustrators of Finding Nemo were about five paces ahead of the scientists who contribute to the Smithsonian.

All of a sudden, a lawn mower engine started and plunged right into my moment under the sea. I was interrupted and had to come back to the surface for a breath of air. There, as the mower continued to disturb, another vision of murkiness appeared. I crawled into a skiff to sail into the hazy world in which we live. I saw the sinister disrespect of children to their parents. I saw the gloomy lack of parental love withheld from their children. The current took me down the shore of corruption, political and economic turmoil, and hatred. I caught the smell of dead fish in the wind- the smell of apathy and revelry. I saw shipwrecked the marriages of over half of our population. I saw, sunken, the ships of over 50 million babies lost to abortion.

It was then that I realized how each of us have so much in common with the spookfish. We are trapped in the depths of a fallen world. According to scripture, this world, will grow darker still. We are reliant, like the spookfish, only on the "light" that comes from Jesus. Our trust in him is our life raft and our anchor. We must let the Word of God illuminate our paths and charter our course. Our eyes are the windows to the soul. If the eye be filled with darkness. How great is that darkness!

Nonetheless, whatever problems we may face, I am confident that God's light will reach us. Despite the lonely times trapped under the sea of life, God's light will not only span there, but it will be reflected through us. I am sure that the spookfish cannot see itself and what it looks like to other creatures. We too, have no idea how our light, although a glimmer, gives bioluminescent charges to the blind ones swimming by. Don't think that because you are in obscurity that you are blind and handicapped. Your purpose is for God's reflection to flash all around.

May you and I be content to be totally handicapped by our dependency on Christ. Keep in mind that Dory said it best. "Wanna know what to do when life gets you down? Just keep swimming. Just keep swimming."

FLOWER BY NAME

I don't mind waiting to the last minute for certain things. But, today started out tough. I was getting ready this morning for the tea that we host for the women at the local retirement home, and I pondered. I had some idea of what I would share but I couldn't get peace. It would be something about Ann Platz's book on encouragement. Our tea is called "A Cup of Encouragement" so I knew I better find some inspiration and fast. Until this time I had drawn blanks.

Aside from the beautiful devotions about various flowers and how women sometimes resemble certain ones in their characteristics and personalities... I really kept getting blank pages. I loved how the author mentioned the stately Magnolia and how her elegance and dignity demands respect. I was enchanted by the idea of the "whispering" violet that speaks softly and gently - never rude or loud. None of this applied to me.

I urged the Lord to give me something for myself and then release me at the retirement home. I thought maybe He would call me something rare and unusual. I had hopes He would reveal some hidden trait of a peony or an orchid - but He didn't. He showed me a vision of a rose stem full of thorns, without the blossom.

I laughed to myself and said, "Great, Lord. That is some encouragement." But to feel Him say anything is encouragement enough. He went on. "You see,"... He said. "You are made with certain thorns and people are forced to handle you delicately. It doesn't discount the strength of your life, nor beauty or fragrance of Me when I cause you to bloom." I pushed deeper for more.

I like what I learned. He had taught me this a hundred times before. If God made the rose and He has made me I cannot compare myself to other flowers in the garden. Does a Pansy poke fun at the Daisy because its petals aren't scalloped? Does a Mum demand the Bluebell to bow to it because it is superior? I love it when God shows me how He sees me. If I use my thorns in the right way I can be a protecting force to those around me instead of building walls and shutting people out.

I asked the ladies at the tea to forgive me for my black fingernail polish and for openly reprimanding our volunteers for talking during my speech. They laughed and said, "She's being prickly...that Rose!"

I am content this afternoon to be named in the Garden of God. I rejoice and embrace the flowers around me. They are full of beauty and perfuming me on to greater blossoms, healthier gardens, and more of the sunshine of God.

Rich Man, Poor Man

Money is a touchy subject. If you have a little you want to keep it and if you don't have enough, you are ever seeking a way to make more. If you have a lot.... well...you are in a very dangerous position according to the Bible. Before you think I am socioeconomically biased let me explain.

When is the last time you heard a good sermon, "How to Hate Your Money?" It is just not a popular preaching position to assume. Perhaps ministers who dare to teach you to hate mammon (money) fear that less of it will come to the aid of their own charities and outreaches that need funding.

Another reason people don't openly talk about how

to hate money is because they are too busy hating YOUR money and hating on wealthy people, instead of learning how to hate their own. I can hear the gasps and the smacking of lips now. Poor people, in general, do a lot of judging of the rich and know exactly how to spend each dime more efficiently than the one to whom it belongs. Some middle class people have also never adhered to Jesus' teaching in Matthew 6:24 that "You cannot serve God and money."

If Jesus taught us that it is difficult for a rich man to enter into the Kingdom of God in Matthew 19:23 then why do we not rush to them and tell them, minister to them, and warn them with love? Have an outreach to wealthy people? I know why most don't. Their wealth makes the average Christian uncomfortable. We either assume they have no needs, are unworthy of our time or we feel insecure about our own financial status; no matter what that status may be.

I want to submit that if you or I have ever judged a person based on their wealth that it is not God's best for us. We are to celebrate others' blessings...and by all means pray for them to make it to Heaven. Jesus said it will be difficult for them to make it in. Do you realize that?

I know ministries that put their neck out there to be available to the rich, to disciple them and pray for them and in return they are accused by others of "pursuing their money." They also lose the normal donor because they assume that the rich bank roll them and support them. May I remind you...it is often the rich who give the least, hence Jesus' warnings. So, the next time you are tempted to point your finger at the rich or the ones who warn them as Jesus commanded, please, first ask God how He feels about the situation. I can promise you He wants them in the Kingdom as much as the poor person.

The love of money is indeed the root of all evil and it only takes about...oh negative ten cents in your bank account, for you to be at risk to be a lover of it.

So, when you remove the tree trunk from your own eye regarding money and its influence over you, you will then be able to plainly see the toothpick in your brothers' eye regarding this topic. Don't assume that all rich people love their money. Some poor people love theirs more.

BOYS WILL BE BOYS

The wild side of boys will always manifest. Church settings cannot even contain it. After church was over I saw a pre-school example of a global truth. Boys will be boys. It was a frigid day along the Gulf Coast so I ran to the car to heat it up before the family finished socializing. I am not as social as my husband is at church. Normally when the service is over - I just want to go home.

This was a normal day. After waiting in the car almost half an hour I spotted the cutest little girl; the same girl that once prayed for her wounded caterpillar when I taught her preschool class. She is such a bundle of joy. This day she was wearing a lightweight parka and the hood was bound securely under her neck. She could barely turn her head. As I gazed at her I saw a flash that came out of nowhere. Then before I could blink little Miss Winter went crashing to the ground like a fell tree in the forest. She had no way of breaking her fall and went down; sideways, stiff, and in slow motion. If not for the grass and the cushiony hood on the parka - we would have needed an ambulance.

There stood her brother who had taken her out. He stood proudly as if he had chopped down a mighty California Redwood. I couldn't believe my eyes at what happened next. Before she had time to wiggle he took three purposeful, giant steps backwards, spread his legs, and threw his head back. Pausing, he began to pound his chest with both fists; gorilla-style.

I began to laugh hysterically but the show wasn't over. As the innocent fur ball on the ground attempted to make a motion to get up...he then proceeded to take three giant steps forward. This is getting good, I thought to myself.

On step number three he did a wax-on, wax-off Karate Kid motion that could have intimidated Bruce Lee. On step three he froze in that position as if daring her to move. She made her attempt to get up and she fell again. Her parka wasn't helping this time. He began to point and laugh and then ran out of sight. The flash was off again to the next victim.

It was a sight to behold. Instantly and through my laughter I was reminded of the book, *Wild at Heart*. I was taken to a place of primitive instincts of the male species I had learned about from the book. There is a basic need for men and boys to hunt, to conquer, and to win.

The problem is that the modern-day warrior is busy trying to conquer all of the wrong things. The real warriors are those who are active and engaged in their own children's lives. A trooper is one who is on full-alert to protect his marriage and guard it from outside forces. The champion is he who prays for and with his family and leads them into the Word of God. A man's sword is the Holy Bible and his only guarantee of winning is through Jesus.

My husband leads a mentoring group for fathers and husbands called: Man Up. I think it is an appropriate name that says it all. If boys and men are truly wild at heart then they need to Man Up with the right things. My husband isn't perfect and he has made plenty of mistakes. But he is still committed and is a great provider.

I am sure that this Karate Kid would not have been as dramatic had he seen his father step in to protect his little sister. I imagine he would have melted his karate chop right into praying hands position. So it is with our men of today. When facing a bad economy, temptations, and a culture that makes it easy to weasel your way out of a marriage...it is time for the men to pull out the gorilla dance if needed. When times are hardest, is when it is time to "Man Up." The Bible is clear that those who do not take care of the needs of their own homes are worse than infidels. This is no gray area. It also speaks about cowards and that they shall not enter into the Kingdom of Heaven. However, I don't think little Mr. Karate Kid will have any problems.

BLEST NEST

I have an affinity for birds. I don't know when it started or why. Perhaps it is because God, Himself, used a bird to send hope to Noah after the flood.

Perhaps it is because the Holy Spirit appeared "as a dove" when Jesus was baptized. God is also like a big bird in a way. He said that He would hide us under His wing and His feathers.

There have been dark times in my life that I have literally imagined, that like a baby bird, I nestled right into the deepest place of God's wing daring someone to find me.

I've been busy working on a project for the ministry that includes a nest as the theme so several nests have come my way. A friend recently gifted me with a beautiful nest full of eggs. Another friend offered a different version – an empty nest. She had watched a bird all spring. It had diligently built a beautiful nest. She had tended it daily. She acted as though she was the proudest and best momma-bird alive. Sadly, she never had any eggs. Ever.

I wonder if this momma-bird (that never was) ever compared her nest to others' or felt inferior. I wonder if she fought back tears, feelings of jealousy or lies that she was a failure.

While working on my front door yesterday (it seems God speaks to me there) I was torn. "Do I decorate with the empty bird home or the man-made-home-décor-FULL-of-eggs one?" I believe that we have nests in our lives too: some empty and some full.

If we focus too long on the full ones we can be fooled into thinking that we have somehow accomplished something grand. The truth is – all good and perfect gifts come from the Father.

If we look too intently on the empty nests and the unfulfilled dreams we may be tempted to become depressed or blame God for not fulfilling our expectations. It is especially hard when we have labored. It's hard to sit on our nest and wait...

If you have an empty nest today I pray that you will

put your trust in God and expect Him to make all things beautiful in its time. He said His plan for you is good; never to harm you.

If your nest is flawless, full, and overflowing maybe it is time to consider the other little birdies that may not have it quite like you.

Take a flight over and lend a song of encouragement to a neighboring nest. But make certain to leave an egg or two or your song will be in vain.

Here's to hope and new beginnings. I chose to decorate with the fake nest and place the real nest for a new bird to find it- open and ready to freely occupy.

Maybe some broken bird needs to catch a break in its life. I pray your nest is blessed today. No nest is sweeter than a generous one.

Umpire of My Intentions

I intended to stop using my personal face book account. Fail. I intended to lose some weight. Fail. Well, you get the idea. What we "intend" to do and what actually happens are altogether different things. Tucked away in Proverbs 25 we see, "Reliable friends who do what they say are like cool drinks in sweltering heat - refreshing! Like billowing clouds that bring no rain is the person who talks big but never produces."

I see this all the time with baseball players. Some guy on the team will inevitably complain that he never gets his chance. These characters are the ones that will also announce that he is better than anyone on the team, yet, when it is his turn at the plate - he strikes out; never producing. My son, Caleb, recently said something after a game. He said, "We executed." I was reminded that it is far better to under promise and then over deliver than the other way around.

Look, I am not happy with myself lately because I catch myself remembering that I said I would call someone back and fail to do so. These small personality flaws add up if they become habits. Can anyone rely on me? Or am I like that billowing cloud? Am I like the whiney, prideful player who thinks too highly of himself? When it is my turn at the plate do I chase the slider, lose my balance and spin around?

Someone said that we tend to judge ourselves on our intentions and judge others based on their actions. I see an umpire in certain areas of my life. He is short, grumpy, and intentional. He stands watching my every move so that he can ring me up and call me out. I don't like to walk back to the bench of my life knowing that I have elbowed for a position that I obviously don't deserve.

I pray that God will help us today to give each other grace when we don't live up to our own bloated expectations and empty promises. I also pray that you and I will be slow to speak. I pray that we will learn to be the reliable friend that can be counted on in a pinch. Let's make of ourselves, by the power of the

Holy Spirit, a great team player that allows our actions to speak louder than our words.

DISNEY REJECTS

It was family vacation and we were headed for Busch Gardens but we got distracted. We passed several roadside theme parks in Orlando. On every corner there was an advertisement for reduced prices to Disney World. There were hundreds of peddlers trying to score off of tourists.

Out of raw curiosity we ventured onto the grounds of one of these "mini-me" Disney Worlds after a stop for lunch. We got what we had coming. It was nothing more than an entrepreneur's attempt to appease the tourists who couldn't otherwise afford the larger theme parks in the city. It was more like a hokey fair. The grounds were laden with "scary people" working the rides; dirty uniforms and dirty mouths were everywhere. We really got a laugh when we encountered casino-type vending machines with knock-off hand bags inside. The guests were stuffing cash into the machine, hand over fist.

The park was filled with drifters and side shows. I can still smell the gasoline fumes from the noisy go-carts. Within fifteen minutes I announced to our group that we had officially become "The Disney World Rejects." Laughingly, we hustled to get out of there before a ride became faulty and hit us or worse - that we caught some disease. It was hideous. We looked around at the other people in the crowded convenience store parking lot and they seemed ecstatic. The theme park junkies seemed to be thrilled with the festivities.

I was disturbed. As I watched entire families run past me and listened to the children squeal with delight...I wondered. Had this corner lot become a deceptive Disney World Mecca? I wondered further if there was a strapped dad within my view who had told their toddlers that they were going to Disney World and this was their big day. I mulled over the idea that this may be the only Disney that they would ever see.

I made a note to myself that day in the Park -for- Rejects (me). We can only long for something more authentic for our lives when we know that something better exists. We must be exposed to the real thing and often, if we are to grow discernment for counterfeits. Likewise, we cannot be disgusted by scams, shams, and knock-offs unless we know a new and improved way of life.

I learned that day that as the real theme parks offer safety, cleanliness and service - so does a life in God.

A life filled with compromise and convenience lands me nothing but phony and second-class living. I don't want to settle for less than what God sent Jesus to provide for me. I refuse to settle for smoky religion and faux promises. Satan and this world's affairs always offer us a counterfeit. I don't have to live with habitual sin. I don't have to live in lack. I don't have to be depressed. As I was thinking these thoughts... a brute tattoo-clad man blew his smoke in my face and blurted obscenities. I made myself this promise. I don't have to be a spiritual reject who settles for cheap thrills. I WILL HAVE THE REAL THING.

I made it a point that day to also never allow those around me to spiritually become duped. I pray that each of us redeem our park passes to God's perfect will for our lives. May we never settle for fake living and empty promises that come from a life of sin. I have no problems carrying a fake handbag or having frugal entertainment in my life. But not for one second should you or I settle for alternate lifestyles that oppose God or anything that isn't authentic in the spirit. I can afford salvation through Christ's sacrifice - it was freely provided to me.

I ask the Lord to bless you today with more under-standing. Understand today that we live beneath our privilege every time that we operate outside of God's mandates. We mount the Ferris wheel of defeat each time we refuse to forgive. We gamble with our very lives each time we willfully sin.

You and I can rest assured that God will withhold no good thing from those who walk uprightly. He wants us to have His name branded upon us forever. So, if you ever see me in my Gucci tennis shoes and wonder if they are real or fake just go study the real ones first and get back to me. So it is in the spirit...

Lighten the Darkness

I sit here in the glow of the Christmas tree lights - alone. I squeeze the warm cup of hot chocolate and listen to the silence and watch the roll of steam rise in front of my eyes. The light from this tree is keeping the entire house from being dark. Yet, all I keep seeing is "darkness" and hearing is "silence."

I have been unable to write for weeks because I have been trapped back there with the miners. You remember the Chilean miners who were underground for 69 days? I wanted to avoid the topic. But I couldn't get away from the mine. Then, just days later another miner group in China (37 people) died in an explosion. A month later, yet, another 29 in New Zealand didn't make it out alive. Their outcome was much different than the group in Chile.

As I sit here in grotesque luxuries I can't help but ask myself, "What is the best gift I can give to those I love? What can I give to strangers for that matter?" I wanted to use this moment to give you truth about eternity; a place where we will be lit up with the record of our life. The ornaments of our works whether good or evil will be on display for all to see. I will not like much of what I see on that day. I, like you, will give an account on Judgment day and will enter into the fate I have accepted or denied. And I will be recompensed, rewarded, and face my consequences.

In the miners' fates God would have us to see the polar opposite outcomes of the potential fates we will encounter. We will be rescued from an eternal darkness, isolation and loneliness into the loving arms of Father God if we have repented of our sin through Jesus. Or, for those who reject Jesus; by words or by their willful sinning after confessing Him- will spend an eternity in torment, pain, and thirst. I am not as spiritual as some people I know. I don't like to be hungry, thirsty, and hot. I especially avoid the oven coils and campfires. I don't like to be burned. I especially don't like the feeling of not being heard by God. To be separated from Him for eternity is unfathomable. The silence, as I sit next to this Christmas tree while everyone else is sleeping, is piercing my soul.

I point out all of this to say that we will one day give

an account of our lives and they will be measured to the holiness of God. None of us will triumph. If we do not have Jesus as our Savior and have had our sin nature changed into a non-habitual lifestyle of sin... we too will be like the Chinese and New Zealanders who were not rescued.

I wish that your life will provide you with the light of Christ; a new nature, where sin does rule over you and that the fruit of your life shows Christ has flooded you. When He said that we would be a new creature our fruit shows that we no longer live the way we once did. I am not saying that we never sin. But sin, according to the book of 1 John, can no longer be habitual. We, now, are able to forgive and love the unlovable. If this isn't evident in your life or mine, we cannot be fooled. We have not been converted. We have a faith that is without works and is dead. It is not enough to say we believe in God. There must be a new nature. It is like having a tree fully decorated but not plugged in. It is worthless and will be discarded and overlooked. Useless.

I ask the Holy Spirit to help you forgive so that you can be forgiven. I pray that if you are bitter towards others that you will realize that you need to be saved from the root that grows to strangle your eternity. We cannot be plucked from God's hands but we can deny Him with our actions and our names can be blotted from the Book of Life. This is the truth, despite what false teaching you have heard.

If you have been afraid to open the package of salvation, I pray that you would do it today. It is a gift that no one deserves or earns. It is simply a gift. This is the best gift I know to give to my friends and family. I am not and have not been perfect since accepting Jesus, but I assure you that I am not who I once was. I don't want to implode or let my stubborn heart keep me from Heaven. I don't want my shame to keep me from sharing this gift with you. Let Jesus wipe off the black smut and ashes from your face and lift you out of the caverns of sin and set your feet in a high place. May He snatch you out of the miry pit and give you eternal life. Eternal light. Eternal hope. Today.

No More Worms

Beauty has a way of catching our attention. It is not often that we are able to look away when a colorful, fluttering butterfly graces our space. The automatic response is to watch until it dances out of sight.

I was reminded this week that when Christ lives in us that we are beautiful beyond description. Others are drawn to the designs and patterns that God has painted upon our lives. Others watch us float by and may not see the full story behind the artwork.

To a non-discerning onlooker it may appear effortless. The butterfly doesn't advertise its former suffering. Before its entire DNA was changed during metamorphosis it was held captive in a tightly confined space known as a chrysalis. It was dark. It was lonely. It was at the mercy of its environment. It was upside down, suspended, and vulnerable.

Before it emerged as an attraction of nature it was actually hideous; an elaborate worm. It sported bulbous lesions on its skin to lessen the chances of being eaten by a predator and was confined to the ground; a dust –eater. Perhaps you can relate. I know I can. Buckminster Fuller said, "Nothing in a caterpillar tells you it's going to be a butterfly."

We would do well to remember that before Christ entered our wormy lives, we too, were captive to the chrysalis of self. Now that we are able to fly and bedazzle this world with a flash of beauty – may we never forget.

The butterfly is dependent upon specialized photo receptors for ultraviolet light in their eyes. These UV light receptors provide the sense of direction they need for guidance. Likewise, we are to follow the light of Christ.

When your fellow butterfly acts like a creep – take it easy and have mercy. He or she momentarily forgot that their DNA has been changed. They no longer have to be a creeper... so lovingly make an allowance. Moreover, when you are tempted to be jealous of the flight pattern of your fellow butterflies – don't forget the lonely, dark path they have endured.

Be encouraged today. If you haven't yet settled into your chrysalis and let the Master artist transform you – go ahead. Why not resign to the fact that you will never get off the dusty ground any other way? You are destined to fly.

I want you to know that if you are currently in your day of transformation and your vision is dim and your hearing is dull... I am peeking in to tell you that your day is near. The day is near that you will flash into the morning sun, full of splendor and beauty. And when you emerge – never forget that before Christ you were without hope, like the worm. Then, and only then, will your true beauty remain.

"To give them beauty for ashes, the oil of JOY for mourning, the garment of praise for the spirit of heaviness; that they may be called trees of righteous-ness." - Isaiah 61:3

PLAGIARIZING GOD

Everyone knows the golden rule and most try to live by it. However, there are some people who could care less about rules, golden, or otherwise. I fit that description occasionally.

While perusing Facebook recently, I noticed that someone I didn't know had re-posted a devotion that I had written. Initially the temptation was to be impressed with myself. Maybe that is how a singer feels the first time they hear their song on the radio. When a stranger begins to share your work it is a huge compliment.

Digging deeper, however, I noticed that my name was

not included nor credit given and I became a little uneasy. As a soon- to- be- author I became somewhat nervous. "Well, isn't the point in writing to spread a message and reach people," I asked myself. I answered with a resounding, "Yes." So I went on reading the posts and all of the comments.

"I would not let my involvement interfere with the larger picture," I told myself. Seeing people acknowledge Christ in those posts should have been a reason to celebrate. But I wasn't prepared for what I would encounter next. The comments turned into praise for the writer's personal sacrifice of time with the Lord. It must have been a love affair between He and said writer to be inspired to produce the devotion. I still was willing to let it go. Then the person who posted my work began to say 'you're welcome' and 'thank you'...passing the work off as their own. And even more hideous is that they pretended they heard the message from the Lord. It felt like robbery and lies. I was mortified.

My shock would only last temporarily. I made a quick phone call to a wise friend who I knew would give me a spiritual chiropractic adjustment. She allowed the Lord to speak through her. I was admonished to never again try to take ownership of something that didn't belong to me in the first place. She said as a sensitive writer or not - Plagiarist sensitive or not, "A rhema word from God cannot be contained," and it cannot be leased, she warned.

If what I had written had truly been inspired of God then let the faux writers emerge. What did I have to lose? It was God's word and not my words anyway so I had become the greater offender. I was passing off something God had said as my own. He cannot be copy written. I was the plagiarist.

It was hard for me but I consented. She was right. My mind flashed back to a loving Corrie Ten Boom, who was imprisoned in a concentration camp for hiding Jews in her home. She never took credit for her bravery and saw civil disobedience while obeying God as normal as breathing. She said, "Anything good in me is on loan from the Lord." Ten Boom would have been the bigger thief for trying to pass her goodness off as her own.

Oh how we can learn from her. I want to encourage you today in the Lord. What He has for you is yours alone. Even if robbers and thieves break in to steal it - your true treasure is in Heaven where it cannot be touched by defiled hands, like mine or yours.

I pray that you store up for yourselves eternal rewards. Don't be tempted, like I was, to be carnally minded. God cannot be contained. May He overflow in you today.

Better than Jesus, Part 1

I was trying to be better than Jesus. Of course I didn't know it at the time, but it would be revealed to me later. You see, I was going through a very difficult time when my neighbor was constantly harassing my children. They were being confronted and reprimanded for playing ball and as the hill would serve them, the ball often rolled into their yard. We built a batting cage to enjoy and hoped it might also limit the number of times the ball would go next door. Then we found ourselves under the threat of a law suit for the batting cage, despite it being in our own backyard. Things escalated when we had the cops called to us for - yes, you are going to read it correctly - for shooting basketball in the cul-de-sac in middle of a summer day! This happened several times and culminated when the neighbor referred to my son as a "Christian" mockingly. Then she resorted to calling him a "Mother of a Something". Except she used the real words. This fifty-something buffoon, yet seemingly sophisticated-type, topped it off by doing a dancing gorilla imitation toward him (he was only 12).

We ended up pressing charges. When the case made its way to court, the inexperienced city attorney never called our other witnesses and closed her arguments before ever asking my son if she said those things to him. Our verbal abusing neighbor, on the other hand, had a hired attorney that reminded us of a grizzly Mr. Noodle. He relished in his witnesses' lies and spin. Needless to say - she was found "not guilty." Did this Judge's ruling change the truth of what really happened? No. Did I feel for a moment that God had surely allowed justice to fall in the street? Of course. And I was willing to take matters into my own hands. And so I did.

I came home from court ready to avenge my children. I started documenting all behavior. Building my case became my focus. I even had a law firm eager to take the case, pro bono, to seek recompense for my family. Until one day, a friend of mine stopped by to pray with me. She started her prayer with the intention (I had hoped) to pray against my neighbor and that God would move them out of our neighborhood. Honestly, I would've been fine if He would have chosen to move them to another state or country. After all, we were ministers of the Lord and this type of behavior shouldn't be allowed to happen to us, right?

Well, my friend began to pray and before I knew it... she was petitioning God for all sorts of blessings of mercy and grace. She prayed that love from strangers would be poured out on my neighbor. She began to weep and I, well, I, became angry. She prayed harder. Meanwhile, my anger grew. "Lord, promote them on their jobs," she cried. "Give them financial stability..." It went on and on. I, on the other hand, felt betrayed and told God I would not participate in the prayer. My friend then said the words that will forever convict me. "Lord, it is because of your goodness that men are drawn to repentance," she sobbed. I instantly had a vision of the Judge's mouth as she had formed the words, "Not guilty." It became clear to me. That day He manifested His goodness in that verdict - undeserved mercy. I began to weep over God's goodness. He allowed the inexperienced attorney to make a flop of herself. He allowed Mr. Noodle to parade his best game. God, the only true Judge, was, after all...in hot pursuit of my neighbor. His goodness was inescapable.

God was being "good" to her by allowing her to get off scot-free and suffer no consequences legally. He was drawing them to repentance. He knew that He could trust us with the pain of being made out to be fabricators. She on the other hand, needed God to be revealed to her in a major way. I began to weep further over the spiritual condition of a grown woman that would verbally attack young children. I began to see her soul the way God sees her soul. Her soul was at the very least, sick, and at the most....lost and headed for an eternity of separation from Him, unless she turns her life over to Him.

I determined that day to cancel the free lawyers, throw out my scorekeeping notepad and turn it over to The Judge completely. It was clear to me that I had been "kicking against the goads" by opposing her and her foul attitude. I was trying to be better than Jesus. You see, the Bible is clear. Jesus said, "If the world hates you, you know that it hated me before it hated you. If you were of the world, the world would love its own....A servant is not greater than his master. If they persecuted me, they will also persecute you.... they hated me without a cause." I began to embrace the thought of being attacked for prayer. I began to embrace the notion that someone would mock my Christianity. I began to realize that I was striving, as a servant, to be better than my master - Jesus. I repented. I stopped fighting the opposition. I now say, "Bring it on." I want to be in the company of Jesus - persecution and all. And I certainly don't want to pretend that I am better than Him.

Better than Jesus, Part 2

I had a friend who once got blessed with a sharp, new luxury vehicle. She would arrive at work early to park her car in the back parking lot. She would literally pounce onto the pavement and zip across the asphalt to the door. You would have thought there were mud puddles and hail storms from the way she bolted to and from her car. I found out that she did this in an effort not to be seen by her other co-workers. When I asked her why she was behaving so secretly, she said that she didn't want to be questioned about her new car and was concerned that it might make other people jealous. She wholeheartedly thought it would make others feel badly that they didn't have a new car. Her line of thinking troubled me. She thought she was being lowly. In reality she actually had her-

73

self on her mind in excess.

You may recall my former story I shared about my neighbor and how that experience taught me that I would "be better than Jesus" if I didn't accept persecution and hatred as part of being a Christian. That is just one side of the story. I would like to point out that there is another perspective that can easily be overlooked. Allowing our reputation to hinder our Christian position is really quintessential self-centeredness.

There is a thing called false humility. It is when you or I attempt to be humble to the point of transgression. When you or I habitually "stay out of the fight" it reflects a fundamental perversion of what the Bible teaches. We are called to take sides and to take a stance against unrighteousness. Isaiah 1:17 (New International Version)... learn to do right! Seek justice, encourage the oppressed. Defend the cause of the fatherless, plead the case of the widow. (Rebuke the oppressor).

I now recognize that a lot of Christians fail to do this. I, personally, have determined not to shirk my responsibilities any longer. When we neglect to do what the scriptures tell us because it might hurt someone's feelings or look like we are being critical - it is basically pride- reversed and turned inwardly. It does not represent authentic humility. I think we may have neglected this aspect of the Christian frontier.

For instance, if someone crosses a boundary in our lives that is clearly against what our Bible teaches us- why do we park in the back parking lot regarding the subject? Why do we avoid the confrontation? I think it is possible that we are afraid that we will be accused of "showing off" our faith (new car) or passing judgment (where is your new car?). Meanwhile, we are the one trapped in the cycle of "self." My friend was consumed with herself and it led to all kinds of illogical behavior. She tried so hard not to draw attention to herself. The opposite actually happened and her problems only grew. She would never muster the courage to confront her perception of how people saw her. Believe me- when you allow the devil to make you feel guilty for God's blessings... you have problems. It is oppression.

The Bible says that we should speak up for those that cannot speak for themselves, yet, some of us, like my friend, walk in a degree of false holiness causing us to excuse ourselves and turn our heads in every situation. We not only disenfranchise our internal, God-given anger about injustice, moreover, we suppress Godly protest. This is where you and I inadvertently are trying to "be better than Jesus." May I go further? I would dare to say that when we are obliging in our actions when a true injustice has occurred, that God is actually dishonored. I would dare to call it outright, sin. It is outside of the scope of His Word. I know this is a difficult concept. You may have to read it a couple of times for it to penetrate.

Let me tell you what might have prevented the entire escapade with my neighbor. If I would've seen that my children were being harassed undeservingly, I should have been standing on the property line the first time it happened and should have demanded that it never happen again- on the authority of God's Word. I think that is what Jesus would've done. I think that He would have knocked on the door and asked her by what authority was she speaking to the children and remind her of what happens to those who cause an innocent one to stumble. The millstone around the neck story is definitely something we don't want to talk about with a neighbor, right? Why are we ashamed of God's word? He said that not me!

Jesus was notorious for bringing the uncommon forgiveness balanced with uncommon reprimand. He rebuked his disciples when they turned away the little children. Remember? Not only did he rebuke them, He gathered the kids around Himself and publicly embarrassed the disciples by overruling their crowd control measures. Then, Jesus made a display of them further by taking the opportunity to preach a sermon about the importance of children and how they relate to the Kingdom of God. I imagine they were a bit red-faced and humiliated. But, I bet they never made the mistake of turning away children again.

Looking back, I should have stood my ground, too. Firmly yet lovingly, I could have activated God's Word in my life and on behalf of my children. Instead, I chose the popular and overused mentality of "let it go" or "love covers." I learned my lesson the hard way. Trying to be better than Jesus will never bring success.

I don't encourage you to go out looking for a battle. But when wrongdoing shows up at your front door - confront it. Stop pretending that you don't have the Answer. Truth is yours. The Way is yours. The Life is at your call. We have dominion in the earth because Jesus bequeathed it to us.

I am not suggesting that you and I go around pointing out all of the faults of those around us. We have enough of that taking place. But you owe it to those with whom God has called you into relationship. You owe it to them to walk the same line that Jesus did. Don't be selfish or false. Speak the truth in love, because you love, and because you love - you will bring correction when necessary. 1 Corinthians 13:6 says that love, "...does not rejoice in evil but, rejoices in the truth."

Buffalo Chips

As the kids gazed, speechless, at the museum presenter, I watched intently to see what would happen
next. Naomi had just been handed a buffalo chip and
had no idea what it really was. This gentleman obviously had a gift of teaching and it was evident as
he lectured about the great expansion in the Midwest
and how the pioneers lived. The children seemed
transported and were enthralled to learn about more
than just the white man's way of life. They seemed
especially interested in the Indians. Naomi gagged a
bit concerning the deposit she had gotten and then
handed it back to her newest friend. He now had
brought out the rest of the buffalo parts and she was
eager to be "hands-free" for whatever may land in her
hand again. Those buffalo parts seemed to engage

them. Secretly, they engaged me even more.

They learned that most of the structure of the buffalo was used for everyday life. Tendons became string, skin was transformed into clothing, bones were used as plates, horns made nice cups, and even their bladders were salvaged for storing water. That museum presenter didn't know that he had stirred a biblical allegory for me as he taught his passion.

Now back home in my clutter and newest "one button touch" gourmet coffee pot, I keep thinking over how we live in a day of waste and overindulgence. Honestly, I have three coffee pots in my kitchen, not to mention one or two operating ones in storage. As the new year approaches I am thinking of simplifying my life. I don't pretend to aspire to pioneer-style. But, a less-is- more approach seems ideal. However, it feels very complicated to even think about how to tackle the clutter. Because I can't help it, everyday happenstances cause me to think of how the body of Christ is to operate. If we brought all of our resources (clutter) to the table as instructed in the book of Acts, no one would really have a need in the church. I have said it before and I will say it again. In time of economic uncertainty we should barter, give, and bless like never before. It is not only scriptural but good for the environment to recycle, reuse, and reinvent.

Want proof? There was a full two page story on Angelina Jolie giving hand-me-downs to her children.

People magazine actually pictorially tracked how her older children wore the same space invader tees as her now younger children. They called it the "green" thing to do. That should be proof enough. If it works for Angelina, it should work for me and you.

Seriously, I know that we will not resort to buffalo chips as fuel any time soon but the Bible is replete with instructions about doing what is within your power to do - for others. Offering your "extras" to others and being good to those of the household of faith is an honorable thing. It just takes a little extra effort. We, as God's children, have the privilege of offering our gifts and resources to each other and to God's service. We, after all, are the body. In a primitive way, I saw some of these analogies as I saw the buffalo parts and how they were put to use back then. According to the Bible some parts are more comely than others but the less glamorous ones are frankly the more important ones. Don't underestimate the power of what you bring to the table.

Let's keep it simple. You and I can simply our lives by being more generous. "Be" the body of Christ. I will start by asking ~ who needs a coffee pot?

DESPERATE HOUSEWIVES

The age of the desperate housewife did not start with a racy television sitcom. It has been around for thousands of years. For every desperate housewife that has existed, there has been, an equally desperate - househusband. Take our spiritual father, Abraham, for example. He was very busy building altars, protecting offerings, and being God's friend. That may be why he overlooked the problems of his wife, Sarah. She was desperate to bear a child. Despite God's promise to bless them with a child, Sarah convinced Abraham to take her handmaid, Hagar, to expedite things. To set your husband up with your housekeeper in an effort to make God's promises come to life... could be an all- time low. Although, the charades of another desperate housewife, Jezebel, are too numerous for me to mention here.

I wonder who was worse. Was it Abraham, for accepting such a ridiculous offer? Or was it Hagar, for participating in such sin? I think it was Sarah, for orchestrating the whole thing and making the escapade totally accessible. Did Sarah make the bed and put out candles or did she take a girls' weekend trip away from home while the love connection happened? We may never know. The popular term - "desperate housewife" comes to mind as I study their lives. It reminds me how many times I have forced God's hand. In reality, it wasn't His hand at all. It was my hand, my will, my way. Just like Sarah's. I am no different than her. I have made things happen out of time and out of place.

I have also played the role of Hagar, too. I have never been a surrogate, but, I have allowed myself to be manipulated into something that was clearly out of God's will. I think Hagar must have jumped at the chance to show that she could fix the problem. Hagar was at the very least flattered. She asked by Sarah, the richest woman on the face of the earth to fulfill a need. Hagar didn't have a chance. Have I been Abraham? Yes, I have taken an ungodly offer from someone who is supposed to have my best interest in mind. That is where the worst deception can originate - from a perceived Godly person, moreover your Godly spouse.

Take Adam and Eve as another desperate couple. Eve

was not satisfied with the life she was living and became desperate. She was drawn to and became infatuated with - things she did not have. She listened to the lies of the enemy who said that God did not really say what He meant, nor did He mean what He said. Adam did not know how to handle his wife's discontentment and participated in his wife's sin by accepting the forbidden. What kind of man allows his wife to secretly have conversations with a serpent? I think the answer is: a busy man - a desperate househusband. He doesn't know he is a desperate househusband. He may not know that he is married to a desperate housewife. In fact, Adam was walking with God in the cool of the day and naming all the animals. Much like Abraham, Adam had important things to do for God. We should take a lesson from these two families. It has nothing to do with our employment status or our financial status; it looks like it has nothing to do with spiritual to-do lists, either.

When we are so busy with our good works we can often overlook the spiritual condition of our spouse. Their spiritual condition will more than likely affect us no matter how hard we try. We must take "desperate" measures to eradicate the problem of discontentment in our lives and marriages. If Eve and Sarah were victims - who do we think we are? We are desperate housewives in waiting, and if given the right opportunity... the enemy will walk right up to us and occupy. Don't become a desperate househusband, either. If you are not accustomed to telling the people in your life "no" then let this be a warning to you. Abraham could have said, "NO!" Adam could have said, "NO!" (Insert your name here) can say "No!" Say no to desperate attempts to make things happen. Say no to craving more than what God has given you. Say no, especially to the forbidden, if it is brought to you by your spouse. God will honor your position as you wait patiently for the promises.

FREE PASS

Just before school was out I visited my son in his classroom. He had challenged me to come and observe his favorite teacher. I had heard all year about the teaching methods, class humor, and fun. All of the praise was confirmed for me and I agreed wholeheartedly with my son. He had a refreshing learning experience in what was supposed to be a typical day in the life of a pupil. I asked Caleb to stay behind with me after class while I thanked the teacher for the hard work and dedication to the students. My request made Caleb late for his next class so I whipped out a sheet of paper and wrote his Coach a note stating that he had been with me and to allow him to class. I never expected what would happen next.

The teacher looked at my note and then looked at me, obviously a bit confused, then forked out a sheet of paper and wrote, "Caleb Lopes - Pass to class." Instantly, a sinking feeling in my gut caused my head to jerk around, forcing me to take a closer look. I saw immediately how governmental and institutionalized establishments have starved our parental rights. I knew right away that this teacher did not fully understand the extent of parental authority. This teacher was so programmed that even in my presence the obligation to innocently control my son reared its head - trying to override my authority over Caleb. The truth is - this teacher had the best of intentions. The "pass to class" did not disqualify the aforementioned great teaching methods. It did, however, fly in the face of my God given responsibilities as a parent. For a moment, I had forgotten why we have to send our kids away 8 or 9 hours a day to "school" in the first place.

If most parents were able and willing...that burden to nourish our kids - mind, body, and soul, would still fall on us. It was once an honor to teach and train our own children. Unfortunately, today is the day of both parents usually working outside the home. The appetite for higher standards of living drives a money- seeking and money- hungry society. I am not suggesting that all of us who work outside the home are ravenous for money so don't get the wrong idea. I am speaking conceptually here about a greater apathy of parent to child relationships and its apparent nutrient deficiency.

I am convinced that a lot of this same eroding of morals and Christian authority is happening. Although, subtly happening, it is extremely damaging to the spiritual health of the body of Christ. It not only is lying in wait in the educational arena. We wait for the pastor or priest to write us a "pass to class" when we have and have had the authority all along - to write our own ticket - according to the Word of God. Some of us have been passive in our walk with God. We keep sending our kids off to Sunday school believing that they will get all that they need from God in thirty minutes each week. These are nice things to do: church attendance, counsel from elders, etc.

But at the end of the day- the burden is ours and ours alone. The Bible says to train a child in the way he should go and when he is older he will not depart from it. I would like to challenge you and I to scrape every last morsel of the bowl of the Word of God and consume it. Leave nothing behind. Leaving behind leftovers of God's promises is pure waste. Let's frost our kids with the icing of God's Holy Word by speaking it over them. Let's give them their portion of "vegetables" by pointing out when something is out of line and not in accordance to God's order. Stand in the full authority that has been given to you and dispense a well-balanced spiritual meal for your kids.

The truth is, I could have hijacked Caleb that day in his classroom and whisked him away to Jamaica for a half day of snorkeling and a lunch of fried plantains.

Upon our return who would have written his pass to class? Of course it would have been me. I am here to remind you and to write you a free pass, if you will. You have God-given rights and privileges concerning your children. Invoke them. The Lord will honor your faith in Him and His divine recipe for you as a parent.

God of the Gray Areas

It seems as though as things grow more complicated in the world in which we live and so has the
complexity of hearing from God. There are certain aspects of our lives that Jesus did not spe-
cifically address in scripture and we are forced
to come up with some answers on our own.
Have you ever asked God something and He said-----
absolutely nothing? I have. So what's a girl to do when
faced with the decision for pink or red nail polish?
God doesn't care. He likes both colors. He came up
with the idea. The idea of color, that is. I don't think
that He prefers one color to another. When shopping
for your next pickup - Chevy or Ford? God probably
doesn't care about that either.

Wouldn't it be easier if everything were black or white? Some people actually think it is. It makes them feel safer. If everything were black and white then why so many divorces, broken relationships, and failed projects?

The answer is because God gives us choices. Everything is not a science and can't be calculated to the smallest molecule; who you marry, who you befriend, where you attend church, which profession or field you work. More than likely you chose all of these things. Some resolutions are simply left up to us to figure out on our own. Sure, consulting with the Lord is the smartest thing we can do but what if He remains silent?

I once heard someone say that God would have to physically appear to him and speak audibly before he would stop attending the church that his family had been in for generations. This was despite the fact that he was very unhappy, spiritually starved, and hated going each week. Is it possible that he is missing something? I think he is missing a place called - the gray area. That area is a place that some of us never want to venture. Going there- to the gray area- means that we will have to actually trust God with the choices that we make. Without faith it is impossible to please God according to His word. God will not send an answer to every situation so that it is made perfectly clear. He is not always appearing in the form of a burning bush with a voice emanating from it. There are times that the gift of wisdom that He places in us must be utilized. Sometimes it is just good ole' common sense. There are a few people around me and perhaps you know a few of them yourself. They hear a Word from the Lord regarding everything in their life. They are not fooling me. Don't let them fool you, either. Until we see Him face to face will see darkly as in a glass, we know- only in part, and we - the just- shall live by… faith.

We can easily frustrate the grace of God by always wanting a confirmation and a word from the latest and greatest prophet. Don't get me wrong. Some people never ask God's opinion and live in the Land of the Gray, never once asking God for direction or permission. This is not what I am suggesting.

I suggest that you are not reaching your full potential if you have not yet seen the beauty in the fact that God DOES give us choices. If you are a black and white only person…more than likely you could be a bit legalistic, not much fun, living a mediocre life, and are missing so much of what God has for you.

I want to challenge you today to push the limits when it comes to your spiritual life. Get out of the doldrums of the black. Get out of the blandness of the white. Gray doesn't equal rebellion and it doesn't equal confusion. It means that God is quite Big Boy enough to handle your decisions and redirect you if you get off course. Don't let fear of failing keep you from stepping out and doing what is in your heart to do. He is the One who places any good intentions you may have into your heart and mind. You wouldn't think that such an idea originated with you, would you? There is not one good. No, not one. He is the only Good One and He is the God of your gray areas. If... you allow Him.

TRUE BEAUTY EXPOSED

Recently while walking on the beach I had the pleasure of watching a flock of snowbirds strolling alongside me. Snowbirds have a way of being obvious. They are normally senior citizens, appropriately dressed for the beach in the winter. With their hooded jackets, scarves and bags for collecting shells, they swoop onto the sand with intent.

I must have been a stand-out to them. In my Swarovski crystallized ball cap, Roca Wear jumpsuit and matching leather boots to my knees I suppose I was an obvious baby bird. Nonetheless, I got to watch. Each person I passed was painstakingly digging through the sand trying to find flawless shells. I know that's what they were doing because the scarred and broken shells were never touched. Only the ones that appeared to be perfect were picked up, inspected, and then discarded if it had a hole or a chip.

I began to ask myself some questions. What is it with us and perfection? What is our obsession with being unblemished? Who were they to judge which ones were more beautiful? No one had stood at the entrance of the beach with a "snowbird inspection" before allowing them access. For if it were so - some of them wouldn't have passed the test, perhaps.

Before I hit the beach that morning, however, I had just heard a news report about a Hollywood starlit at the young age of 23 who is already addicted to plastic surgery. I don't necessarily like the lines around my smile, but only because someone has told me that they can make them disappear. Do I get a warm and cozy feeling when I look into the mirror and see the bags under my eyes? No. But only because others have theirs disguised or disintegrated. Long gone are the days when a woman looks, with honor, in the mirror and thanks God for the proof-lines in her face that she is still standing despite the blows that life has brought her way. Instead we nip and tuck, laser and suck, inject and augment it all away.

While the waves violently crashed into each other as if fighting for a position... I began to feel sorry for those shattered shells. I also felt pain for the ones who were passing judgment on them. Remnants and pieces of shell were strewn for miles. It was as if I wanted to pick up each one and tell it not to pay any attention to those snowbirds. "Disregard their ignorance for bypassing you or writing you off," I wanted to say. I wanted to remind each one to think back to their glory and beauty of their beginning. I am sure that each one started off intact and full of splendor. I am sure that each one once glistened beneath the sea full of pride and pomp at one time.

The roaring waves, hurricane swells and the predators were sure to blame for any of the marks that I could see on this day. I began to envision the peach colored shell with jagged edges that I was holding had surely been violently attacked by Hurricane Katrina and didn't have a fighting chance to stay lustrous and smooth.

I believe it is so in our lives as well. Jesus said that all those who desire to live godly in Christ Jesus will suffer persecution according to 2Timothy 3:12. The waves will come crashing all around us. Great prideful swells will rise against us. Storms will ravage our lives when we least expect it. The kicks in the teeth from life will chip away at our beauty and scars will be left.

I have a feeling that each shell that got overlooked had a story to tell. I bet each damaged remain from that ocean once had a song to sing. By the looks of them I have a feeling that they had finished their course and ran their race. I empathized and began to identify and honor my own imperfections. I made a decision to somehow accept my smears and smudges as my own proof. I decided that just like those shells-my own brokenness deserves to become very honorable because I am finishing my own course.

I am so glad that the Lord looks on the heart and not the outward appearance. I learned a lesson that day in the cold sand. Each life is valuable despite the rejection from others. The ones that are picked last here on the earth are the ones that God will pick first. That's why I love Him so dearly.

I put into my pocket only two shells that day. I purposely ignored the ones that seemed to have more beauty than the others. Into my Michael Jackson inspired jacket went the darkest stained, knottiest and most scarred ones that I could find. They were actually the most beautiful ones and the snowbirds had missed out. Those shells serve to remind me that charm is deceptive and beauty is fleeting but a woman who fears the Lord is to be praised.

Sign Read, "Colored"

I speak a lot about being an "advancing" Christian instead of a "retreating" one and I often get criticized for doing so. But, tensions are mounting and the stakes are high as we are facing violence, tax funded abortions, and the unraveling of the freedom to practice our faith. Meanwhile, our public schools and government allow and support Planned Parenthood, Muslims, WICCA, and Atheism, which all happen to be faiths in their own right.

My husband Hugh and I recently had a devotion where we were comparing modern day history makers with people in the Bible. There are a few brave revolutionists who put their foot down at pivotal times in history and snapped a chalky plumb line of righteousness. One of them that impressed us the most was Mrs. Rosa Parks.

It has been grossly misrepresented that she sat in the WHITE section at the front of the bus and got arrested for doing so. The truth is...she was sitting in the COLORED section of the bus. She refused to give up her seat that was demanded by a white man.

I envision Miss Rosa that day. When told to move, perhaps trying her level best to hide her fear, pointedly leaned forward to look intently at the sign near her. The sign read, "COLORED." Perhaps she then sat back slowly, seemingly confident in her seat, and shook her head to disagree with him. I think she locked eyes with him to see him in for the surprise of his life. How embarrassing to be refused by a woman (and a colored woman at that). I can hear the thump of the plumb line at her feet and see the cloud of chalk filling the air as it rose from her dusty shoes, swirled around her manicured and handcuffed-bound hands, as the chalk encircled her chocolate hair.

I laugh out loud to think of what kind of guts that woman must have had. Was it raw nerve? Or was it the grace of God? I believe God imparted supernatural strength to her to sound an alarm for - some who would not- and those who, could not - speak for themselves.

Can you imagine how the passengers on the bus that day must have felt? Oh what discomfort and confrontation. I can just see the scowls on the faces of the other white men as she refused to give up her seat. The gasps. The clamor. Can you hear it? I'm sure that the cold air became increasingly noticeable as the bus stood still. I can smell the engine's exhaust - invading; the anxious bus driver becoming agitated. Cars outside the window were still zipping by. They, however, were going nowhere. Or were they?

I can see another black woman whispering to her, "Negro, please, just get up! I'm tired. I've been working all day and I just want to get home to my folks. Are you crazy?" I can barely see a black child sitting next to her tugging her dress hem, "Miss Rosa, please, I'm afraid." I can hear the pulsing curses and jeers from the white teenage boys, laced with the hurling, high-class insults and spittle from the white ladies wearing their perky hats and white gloves. Still, the bus was motionless.

May I suggest to you that we too, are facing some injustices today. Injustice that will leave us motionless if we dare confront them. We may have our evening plans put on hold as we are forced to look truth and lies square in the face. That is, if, we are courageous enough to lock eyes with them.

We may not see immediate result of our efforts. After all, Miss Rosa was thrown in jail that day. But, because of her audacity, our children are reaping the benefits. Her bravery blazed a path to change in our history. What we choose to do today, moreover, what we choose not to do....will have a direct effect on generations to come. Continue to be bold. Stare your accusers and bullies straight in the face. Those who mock your faith, especially. Those who deny your rights- challenge them. Now is not the time to retreat but to advance. Find your God-given boundaries in Christ and guard them.

Believing with you and may we not rest until justice rolls down like the water and righteousness like a mighty stream.

TEA TIME WITH MISS B

As I approached high tea the other guests were wearing their Sunday best and crested with their classy, oversized hats. I began to take note of the details of the room. The Grand Hotel in Point Clear, Alabama has a reputation of being host to some of the finest events in the south. This day, however, had a certain feeling in the air. The tea room was adorned with the typical tea time trays, vintage pots, and centerpieces. The silverware had a special sheen and the chocolate on the strawberries had a design that shouted to us to take notice of how much attention had been paid to it. As we nestled into our seats, the servers began to bustle to make sure the sugar cubes and scones were perfectly placed. It was the ideal setting for a high-class practice session of nose lifting.

I have never been fond of "fancy attitudes" even though I love a fancy outing occasionally. Despite the room full of flawless, lipstick- adorned women there was a feeling that I just couldn't shake. The feeling was mischievousness. The woman to my right skipped the creamer for her tea because, "You are not supposed to drink creamer in hot tea," she reprimanded. "I took tea in London recently and this is a no-no." I answered by tipping the creamer for a second time, filling my orange-infused tea to the brim until it looked like coffee, gave it a swirl, and smiled. I looked over at my daughter, Naomi, to see her drawing instructions from the more mature ones seated primly at our table.

I was sure she had noticed my rebellion with the creamer but she didn't. She had her eyes fixed upon a stranger across the table. This stranger had a sweet demeanor and she was fumbling around with her camera. We all know that you don't "fumble" at the high tea table. I could tell by Naomi's expression that she wanted to lend a hand. Taking silent instructions from the youth and innocence of Naomi, I rose from my seat, and marched right over to offer to take the photo she wanted. Another wave of whatever was in the air rose over us as she breathed out a sigh of relief and told us how she wanted to capture the moment. I admitted to her that I would love for her to return the favor for me as I had not brought a camera.

Miss B, as she called herself, thanked me for the snapshots and then spoke out about how she wished she had worn a hat. Her friend seated next to her, being an artist, took the sheet of paper that the program was printed on and began folding it into the perfect little picture of a hat. Yep. We had went beyond breaking the rules. In the midst of passing cucumber sandwiches, lemon curd, and clotted cream, we began passing the unexpected. When Miss B couldn't get her new paper hat to stay in place I committed high treason of high tea. I reached right over into Naomi's hair and stole a bobby pin out of it! I had officially become Miss B's coiffeur. You should have seen the faces of the ladies to my left when I sent it on down the line so that Miss B could pin her paper hat it into her hair. The lady to my right must have thought we were from Alabama or something. She may have taken tea in London but I was out for a good time. Miss B had inadvertently given me permission.

Then I noticed Miss B's eyes. She was fixed on the centerpiece. It was a magical tea cup and saucer brimming with the finest flowers that Spring had to offer. I read her mind - then pounced. I jerked a white daisy from it and passed it along. Miss B had the prettiest smile I think I have ever seen and it only grew each time we exchanged our mischief.

Our table turned into a joy feast as Miss B opened up to tell us that the pictures were for her blog about turtles. We had met the Turtle Lady. She writes about them and their imaginary relationships with God. She also learned that she had worn paper hats to events in the past. This was not new to her. We began to laugh out loud and got to know each other in the spirit of fun. I would say that more than the ice was broken. We broke through the stereotype of a fancy affair and actually got to each other's hearts. Before I knew it Naomi was asking for more sandwiches. You could tell that everyone was relieved that she had asked for seconds because they were allowed to participate in more of the pass-arounds. We were all secretly starving and were all afraid to push politeness aside to quiet the growling from our stomachs.

What was staged for a stiff-necked affair turned out to be a sincere exchange of love. The camera and paper hat that day served us better than the white glove service we received. It opened up a floodgate of laughs, story-telling, and gave the permission slip to Miss B - to be..... herself. What we would have missed if we had been too busy with our teaspoons and cups to take note of each other.

I think this is the same with our everyday lives as Christians. We can get so engrossed in our outward appearance, our protocols, and our traditions that we miss the heart of God altogether. I am so proud that I saw Miss B's heart as I was taking my tea. I haven't had that much fun in a long time. Thank you, Miss B for reminding me that I don't have to be "formal or fancy" with God. I lift my pinkie finger to you and to my other friends to say that God is in for a good time, as well. He loves you. He adores you. He is willing to overlook your manners if you are willing to sit at the table. Who cares if you accidentally make a mess or say the wrong thing? He doesn't even mind turtle talk. He wants to fellowship with you so that you can get to know Him better. He already knows about you completely. Be yourself with Him and get close to His heart today.

THE DEVIL'S WATER BOY

The movie, *Water Boy*, has an alligator-eating main character named Bobby. He is a mama's boy and his eccentric and overbearing mama is obsessed with the devil. Or as she pronounced it, "the debil." At every turn in the movie she cites the personality from hell for anything bad. Bobby's emotional conflict (EC) or his learning disability (LD) would probably be attributed to his mother and would be listed this way in his Individual Education Plan (IEP). I use special education terms because it is the language educators use when referring to students by their diagnoses and how they must document certain behaviors and develop a plan based on the educational goals. If I were Bobby's educator I would have to come up with a way to work around his frequent visions and hallucinations. In this movie, which I do not recommend, Bobby is haunted by visions of her favorite words, "That's from the debil!"

Our Individual Education Plan ideally is to follow the Bible, imitate strong Christian leaders, and see an impact on other people's lives. However, much like the children with disabilities or the children that are gifted are in special education programs there still will be inherent flaws. As educators do their level best to see the student succeed and have legal documents detailing a plan and a course of action for set goals. We, too, have plans that sometimes get clouded by leaders who fail or by fables or myths handed down to us by otherwise spiritual people. I know that as Christians, some of us could use a modification in our spiritual IEP's. Like Bobby, a lot of us think that the devil is responsible for so much, when in fact, most of our problems are the result of our own choices. The devil has nothing to do with it! I say this with caution as I know some fellow Pentacostal will throw stones at me.

Once I had the privilege of ministering to a group of girls at Mercy Ministries, a home for troubled girls. Well, troubled is a gracious way of putting it. Most of the girls that land in Mercy are given up on by the mental health clinics and sent home to die. Most are eating disorder cases, cutters, and addicts. I will never forget some of the looks on their faces when I shared this perspective with them. Most of the bondage that they have encountered was embraced by their own free will - one decision at a time. Just like yours. Just like mine. In fact, I would venture to say that if you are cheating on your spouse, the devil really didn't make you do it. You used God's greatest gift to you to fall, you used and exercised your own free will. You and I have options daily according to scripture, "I have set before you this day, life and death. Choose life...so that you and your children may live." No devil intervention needed.

God is so in tune with the free will notion that He didn't stop Lucifer from exercising his free will in Heaven. Remember? He, the anointed music and worship leader, decided to overthrow God. He said, "I will ascend my throne above God's." Then in a fiery flash of lightening God gave him what he wanted and kicked him out of Heaven and Lucifer had now become Satan, Beelzebub, Prince of Darkness, the Devil, the Debil. Pick your poison. He got what his freewill decisions handed him. He got a home called Hell and a host of fallen angels called demons to help carry out his work.

So, the next time you see someone wreaking havoc be very careful before you give too much credit to the Adversary. I know that he is a deceiver and a liar and places real bondage on people who need deliverance by a touch from God. But never forget that he can never ever touch someone without God's permission or by an invitation by the person who opens the door by sin in their life - one choice at a time. Don't be as pea-brained as Bobby and his mama to say, "It's the debil!!!" Let's upgrade our Christian IEP's with personal responsibility, solid Bible teaching, and holy living. Let's use our freewill for more than "fetchin' water" and we will begin to see more and more positive changes in our lives.

Toothpick Trees

It was brought to my attention lately that sometimes religion can influence how we view other members in the church. I wanted to share St. Paul's view about himself as a leader and his view about those who are called to lead others to Christ.

"Dont imagine us to be something we aren't. We are servants of Christ, not his masters. We are guides into God's most sublime secrets, not security guards posted to protect them. The requirements for a good guide are reliability and accurate knowledge. It matters very little what you think of me, even less where I rank in popular opinion. I don't even rank myself. Comparisons in these matters are pointless. I'm not aware of anything that would disqualify me from being a good guide for you, but that doesn't mean much. The Master (God) makes that judgment.

So don't get ahead of the Master and jump to conclusions with your judgments before all the evidence is in. When he comes, he will bring out in the open and place in evidence all kinds of things we never dreamed of - inner motives and purposes and prayers. Only then will any of us get to hear the "Well done!" of God.........for who do you know that really knows you, knows your heart? And even if they did, is there anything they would discover in you that you could take credit for? Isn't everything you have and everything you are sheer gifts from God? So what's the point of all this comparing and competing? You already have all that you need. You already have more access to God than you can handle...youre sitting on top of the world- at least God's world- and we are right there, alongside you!" 1 Cor. 4 The Message Bible

Every leader in the body of Christ, including you, has great secrets to share from the Lord. Likewise, we all have flaws that keep us humble and reliant upon Jesus. I pray that you will always be quick to share your God secrets with others and that you will also be cautious to compare others to yourself. I love what Jesus said to the Pharisees, "First remove the tree trunk from your own eyes so that you can clearly see the toothpick in your brother's eye." It is, indeed, the ones who are blinded by telephone poles (stuck in their eyes) that love to point out the splinters in everyone else's lives. I pray that is not you. I pray that is not me.

So off I go now to till and garden - working on up-rooting the Live Oak growing in my own eyes. I have loads of work to do.

GOD OF THE SECRETS

Ever had a secret? Ever had a dark, dirty one? I have. It can be one of the most exhausting of all feats - to attempt to keep a secret hidden. There are some things that you pray no one ever discovers about you now or about your past.

A man named Achan buried his secrets under his tent. It almost worked until the time came that God wanted to put His finger on it and exposed it. Achan had taken some things from the treasures of the city of Jericho when it had been overtaken. He can be quoted as saying, "When I saw among the spoils a beautiful Babylonian garment, two hundred shekels of silver, and a wedge of gold weighing fifty shekels, I coveted them and I took them. And there they are, hidden in the earth in the midst of my tent, with the silver under it."

I often wonder what Achan was going to do with the goods. After he buried them under his tent what a morbid relationship he must have had with them. Maybe he would go to the spot when everyone was sleeping and see the fresh mound of dirt, give it a pat and feel secure that it was still there. He wasn't even able to spend the silver yet it somehow made sense to him to keep it in his possession.

I imagine that he occasionally unearthed his secret and lifted the 50 pound bar of gold, stroked it, and then used it like a mirror to see himself in the beautiful robe. I think he sat there Indian-style, wearing the robe, admiring himself until reality arrived with the footsteps of people outside his tent. Struggling and with tired forearms he probably had to hurry and put it back into the ground. How did he hide the sound of it touching those silver coins? Not to mention the dirt that must have gotten under his fingernails each time he secretly played with his skeletons in the closet.

I am sure he was haunted by the guilt of it. The spot where he buried his secrets was no doubt softer ground than the rest of the square footage under his tent. I'm sure that each time a family member walked there they rocked back and forth asking themselves *what is that funny feeling under my feet?*

It isn't much is different for us. When we harbor a secret it calls out to us from deep beneath the earth -reminding us that it is there and demanding our attention. It can never be silenced until it is dug up, exposed, and then utterly destroyed.

I have determined that I will surrender my secrets on my terms and not on someone else's. Unlike Achan, who was forced into the public light and his entire family destroyed... we have different options. God's grace is here for us for forgiveness and for mercy. If we choose to run to Him with palms up - full of our dirt and baggage - He is on hand to heal us. If we keep them hidden and think we can outsmart God - we will one day be put on our ear and all of our bags of bones will be brought to the surface and put on display for the entire camp to see.

I pray that you will run into the Arms of Mercy. His name is Jesus and He is ever ready to conceal your secret if you are honest with Him. He loves you today.

SECRET STAR

I was told by a very dear friend that God spoke to her heart about how stars are always shining whether we recognize them or not; and how the daylight sun overshadows their brilliance so that we cannot see them. She made a correlation about the body of Christ being like stars. It made me begin to ask myself some hard questions. Who do I know that lives a life that "shines" but never gets the recognition they deserve? Several people came to my mind. These people do things under the radar and behind closed doors perhaps by writing a letter or visiting someone in need - when no one else is looking.

At first I wanted to print up an appreciation list and put out an ad in the newspaper to speak of these STARS who go unnoticed... but then I began to hear a different story in my heart. God began to show me a picture of the many times that my own good works have been put on display, placed in the spotlight, or touted by men. I felt a sense of loss rush over my entire being. Not that what I did was bad. Not that those who recognized me were bad, either. It's just that something was final about it. Nothing eternal would ever come out of most any of it. I had read about us suffering loss when we meet Jesus and I pressed harder for an answer.

Then the Lord took me to Matthew 6:1-4. "Be careful not to do your 'acts of righteousness' before men, to be seen by them. If you do, you will have no reward from your Father in heaven. So when you give to the needy do not announce it with trumpets, as the hypocrites do in the synagogues and on the streets, to be honored by men. I tell you the truth; they have received their reward in full. But when you give to the needy do not let your left hand know what your right hand is doing so that your giving may be in secret. Then your Father, who sees what is done in secret, will reward you."

I wonder how many eternal rewards I have unknowingly lost? For instance, the times I have been listed in the program or the check presentations with photo ops, and not to mention the trumpeting social media updates, alone. Wow...what an empty reward. When the day of testing comes and I stand before the Throne of God for my works to be tried in fire...none of those good things will go with me into eternity. They will simply burn away because they were not done in secret.

I share this with you so that perhaps the next time you serve someone in need or serve an organization maybe you will consider my loss and not make the same mistakes. You are a shining star in the Kingdom of God whether anyone recognizes you or not. If you have gone totally unnoticed then you may be in the best position of anyone, eternally speaking. Keep shining - secretly - and you will have your reward where it really matters.

God Sabotages My Prayer

Last night while saying my, Now-I-lay-me-down-prayers, I got frustrated. I had made my typical "I'm sorry list" to God. But, as I prayed, the list seemed to get longer and longer. Making sure not to overlook any bad behavior I began to pick apart my day.

I confessed how bad I felt for hanging up on the lady at the bank and for calling the woman on the road an idiot. Then I thought about the comment I made here and there; so on and so forth. Finally, the Lord politely interrupted me and asked me if I had the time to actually recount the endless offenses. I was stunned.

I realized that He, indeed, had the time but was being a gentleman to me. He then told me that I should probably just confess that my heart had developed an ungodly attitude. He went on to tell me that He was quite capable of handling the details. My play-by-play commentary was unnecessary.

I paused and questioned Him as to why I shouldn't tell him every rotten detail of my day. It was evident. He was not interested in my conscious-easing session that I was mistaking for prayer. He reminded me that if I confessed my sin (bad attitude) that he would forgive me. Forgive me He did, and that was the therapeutic exchange.

I had somehow discounted the power of His forgiveness, unknowingly. I took the burden of conjuring up every sordid detail, which happens to be a work of the flesh. He reminded me 1Samuel 16:7, "The Lord does not look at the things man looks at. Man looks at the outward appearance but the Lord looks at the heart." (NIV) The outward things whether good or bad will be judged based on our heart condition at the time. Purity of heart and motives will all be tested and only He knows a man's heart.

So, here I am, to remind you of the same. God knows your heart even better than you and it can be trusted with Him. Don't neglect to confess your sin, but remember, only He is capable of counting that high.

It's Never "Just Lunch"

It has been many years ago but I still get excited when I think about it. Hugh, my husband, and I would be having lunch with two of the most influential people in America as it relates to ministry. Not to mention that they are both also best-selling authors with years of experience and a large field of wisdom in which to glean. Why had I been invited? I couldn't put my finger on it and made the mistake of asking the question aloud.

I didn't see it coming. The person I confided in unknowingly knocked the breath out of me with her words: "Why does everything have to be spiritual for you? Jennifer, ITS JUST LUNCH!" Of course, she didn't know that she had just thrown a powerful uppercut. Those words injured me and sent me to my corner, never wanting to return to the ring. I can't blame her because I should have had a counter move and defended myself. I should have opened my mouth and punched back at the doubt and unbelief... but I didn't. I let those words replay in my head a thousand times. I am not the type of person that has time for "just lunch" and want every action I take to be full of meaning and purpose. Each time I played the record "IT'S JUST LUNCH" I began to doubt myself. "ITS JUST LUNCH" was the new #1 hit and everywhere I turned it was playing. I began to fear that I wasn't even called into the ministry at all. In fact, I was crippled for almost two years and couldn't move forward. And it was her face and her words that appeared to me.

In life it isn't the offenses that come that are so threatening but our reaction to them. Jesus said that these offenses would come. I've since learned that what people say and do is a mere reflection of their own values and beliefs and we can't absorb them for ourselves. If what someone says doesn't line up with what we know for sure God has shown us then their words are a threat to our faith. I had given this person too much influence in my life. I had an unhealthy respect for her viewpoint and didn't realize it.

If we value too heavily what any one person says it can harm us. God forbid they offer selfish advice or ask questions out of their own personal agendas. Where does that leave us? It leaves us with spiritual broken ribs, gasping for air when doubt sets in. I am wiser now. I know that nothing ever JUST happens. God, Himself, is the Orchestrator of my life: every event, happenstance, and person in it isn't by CHANCE. God orders my steps and is weaving a pattern and theme for my today; for my future. I don't shuffle weakly back to my corner anymore. There is too much on the line in this Championship fight for Christ. I don't throw in the towel. I fight harder. If you have had words spoken to you that caused injury – fight back. Don't attack the person but attack the concept behind the words they used. Don't absorb their contradiction to God's best and highest for your life. That is why I now have a corner full of people that speak words of life and faith. It is round two. Ding. Ding.

MY ANNOYING FRIEND

Ever been haunted by that one "annoying" friend? I think everyone has one. You know - the kind of friend that no matter where you turn you can't escape.

This particular friend of mine was facing a crisis in her life. She was given uncertain news from the doctor concerning her child. I quickly discovered that when you love someone their crisis also becomes your crisis. She became annoying and rather quickly.

At one point she needed a wheelchair in order to maneuver comfortably during the late stages of her pregnancy. All hands were on deck to make sure she was comfortable. However, she began to use the strength she had left to serve others. Enter irritation. The phone call came that sounded like sandpaper to my ears, "Can you go with me to the hospital? I want to visit a friend who has a sick baby." I, however, wanted to sleep in. Thereby, she became... annoying. Not only did I want to sleep in that day but the very core of my self-preservation was challenged by her request. One excuse after another flooded my mind. You are pregnant. You often need a wheelchair. The condition of your unborn is uncertain. But she gave me no excuse. She was determined. If she had no excuse then why did I look for one?

This behavior only escalated. She began to creatively search out ways to be a blessing to others while facing perhaps what might be the darkest days of her very life. I saw total peace in her heart and an authentic fervor for others. She insisted on hosting a gathering at her home to put a few worried people at ease. Isn't this a picture of what Jesus would do? Jesus led his disciples by example. He came to serve and not to be served. He went out of His way to be unpredictable with His extravagant pursuit of people.

My friend has helped me in many ways with her both-ersome-to-me behavior. She irritated me because she challenged my level of selfishness. I had full strength and health yet I was apathetic about outreach. Meanwhile, while she faced a crisis...she was vigilant to serve others. There remained no justification for my level of laziness. I have since realized that her fierce pursuit of others has allowed me to be honest with myself. Her life was a blazing display of the glory of God at work. At the very core of our own disappointments, fears, and pain we must elicit a force that is greater than ourselves. Love pursues. Love risks rejection. Love presses into the dark places. Love isn't self-centered.

I am thankful for my Annoying friend and her example in my life. I will treasure those moments of being challenged on the inside to rise a little higher and to show love in tangible ways. I have seen her beautiful example of what it means to rise higher by bending lower to properly serve others. If ever I can create an irritation that elicits this prodding in others then I will be able to call it a great day.

It's long been said that we are blessed to be a blessing. And now I know even when we don't feel blessed, we have the power to still be a blessing.

FALL BLOWS IN A LITTLE DECEPTION: RESISTING THE WHITEWASHED TOMBS

We have all heard the advice to never judge a book by its cover. While cleaning my house today I caught a glimpse of the orange, purple, and lime green swags of ribbon-netting above my front door. I could see the colors beaming in the sunshine through the window overhead. All of a sudden I imagined if I didn't live in my home and only saw the beautiful door-scape from the outside; what I would think about the people inside. The whitewashed tomb began to conflict with my imagination.

I began to imagine myself on the outside and smells seeping from around that door of freshly baked apple pie. I imagined the lady of the home churning homemade, vanilla- bean ice cream to put atop. My mind was filled with a vision of an apron clad domestic diva that could commandeer that home behind the glimmering door. All of a sudden I realized that the "diva" was me. What a wake-up call. I do get caught wearing a cute apron occasionally, but, not for the aforementioned reasons. But, I am no apple-pie-baking diva, at all.

In fact, I don't have many skills in the kitchen. The woman in my vision wasn't wearing black toenail polish and she wasn't still seeing the orthodontist as an adult. This woman in my daydream was more like Harriet from the old television program, Ozzie and Harriet. She was wearing a pencil skirt and pearls. There is a slight problem. I don't know Harriet and the only Ozzie I know is Ozzie Smith. I looked over at the photo of me with Ozzie that is perched on the writer's desk in my kitchen and I was jolted back into reality. I can cover up, paint up and even try to cook it up. But at the end of the day...I will still be what God made me to be.

I came to a strong conclusion in that moment. We can really, sincerely, genuinely never... ever get caught judging the book by its cover. Appearances can be so deceiving. I often think of a woman in all her glory. I imagine that after she disrobes from the latest designer fashions, jewelry and heels then one can focus on her, alone. When the make-up remover is applied it is no problem for her; at least she still can rely on the hair. What happens once the hair falls flat and is pulled into a ponytail? Wait. There is still the lingering Botox. But let's pretend it has expired and she is left totally exposed. Will she still be viewed as beautiful?

I would hope that her beauty exudes from within and that the answer would be "yes." However, I dare say that many men are left feeling duped and wondering how they got tricked once all the cards are on the table. Or shall I say...off the table.

So I decided today to rat on myself. If you or anyone you know ever comes looking for a hot meal from my house...don't be fooled. My front door would portray that I am the domestic diva. But you better pick up the take-out on your way here, lest you starve.

This is true for some people who claim to be Christians. Matthew 23:27 speaks of men who are like whitewashed tombs. They look beautiful on the outside but on the inside are full of dead men's bones. Jesus warned these folks needed a clean-up, from the inside-out. Attending church and having a "God bless you" on your lips isn't a qualifier. What do you have on the inside? In the end it is all that really counts, anyway. Have we given Him lordship over our lives?

I pray that your heart is yoked to Jesus and that your insides tell a story of beauty and matchless destiny in God. May the "door" of your heart be opened to Him, continually. In the meantime I will keep decorating the door and busting down the walls - the white-washed tombs of deception.

And for the record: tonight...if it isn't delivery, it's Digorno!

Just A Note

I sometimes panic when I realize I haven't written a thank-you note to someone. I am not very good at it and am working harder at stewarding relationships. It is very important that we let others know of our gratitude.

I sat listening to worship music this morning and I felt impressed that I should write the Lord a thank-you note. I sat, motionless, wondering how to approach such a task. It then occurred to me that like any other relationship, He longs for me to affirm Him. Not that He needs it, but that I do. I need to acknowledge the things He does for me on a daily basis. So, I thought I would share a portion of my note to Him.

❧

Dear Jesus,

My hand hasn't the power to create, nor form a word that would describe Your Goodness. Although You invented the spoken and written word I must rely on You to help me. So, I press this pen into this paper as a symbol of my praise to You. With each stroke of ink I am aware of the way You send messages to me each day.

Like yesterday when You sent someone to Bible study when there wasn't a Bible study scheduled. How You used her simple knock at the door to affirm that You have called me into ministry and that every seed of doubt that has been planted is being uprooted. Like Round-Up, upon my fears -you sprayed your holy presence on the toxic words of the past. "Have you really been called to ministry?" Today, Lord, those words are brown and wilting and soon will be fallen weeds in my life. Thank you.

It would be impossible to tell You of Your great wonders. So I must trust in the knowledge that You, alone, are the only One capable of knowing. Moment by moment You flood my life with perfect peace. You are higher than any word and are not bound by my expressions. In Your perfect love for me I will never possess the ability to thank You properly. But as long as I have breath I will attempt to do it anyway.

Your Daughter,
Jennifer

I challenge you to try writing a thank-you note to God. See what happens. Once a day, for one week, get the best stationary available to you. Even if it is mere notebook paper - it doesn't matter. Write the Lord of the Universe a note. I can promise you this: He will respond.

Job's Friends - Our Friends

Satan showed up for the meeting with God. God then posed the question, "Have you considered my servant, Job, that there is none like him on the earth... upright, fears God and shuns evil?" Then Satan basically said, "This is true only because you bless him and have him protected. Take away what he has and he will curse you to your face."

God took the challenge from Satan and told him, "Go for it. Wreak havoc and touch whatever you want but do not touch his life." If you don't believe me read it for yourself. There is a whole book in the Bible dedicated to this meeting.

I often think of Job. But, more often, I think of his friends. When Job was facing his darkest days his friends began to blame him. They tried to pin him with sin because of the chaos that was happening in his life. The missing element is that they were clueless about the meeting and God's proposal to Satan. God issued permission; therefore, Satan took full advantage. He devoured everything.

Job lost his money, his possessions, and everything he owned in one day. Because of this, Job's friends began to concur with these types of announcements: "Something must be wrong in your life." You are a sinful man." How wrong they were.

Job's friends were clueless. They had a form of godliness but that was all. They knew the scriptures but lacked an intimacy with God, unlike Job. They memorized scripture but didn't know the God of the scripture.

God wanted to prove to Satan that there was such a man that would still honor and serve Him despite affliction. Is it possible that a loving God would allow pain to enter our lives so that Satan can get another "loss" on the score card? I submit to you – yes. When you compete against someone do you play merely to win? That is one -sided. It means that the opponent loses. Their loss is a factor in your competition; or else you would stick to playing Solitaire.

The difference for us, now, is that Jesus is seated at the right hand of the Father, interceding for us. We now have a high priest who prays for us when this happens. Maybe God brings up your name at a meeting. This is what happened to Simon Peter. "Simon, Simon, Satan has asked for you...to sift you as wheat, but I am praying for you, that your faith faileth not."

Imagine for a moment Jesus speaking to you. "Insert your name here... Satan has asked for you to sift you as wheat, but I am praying for you, that your faith faileth not."

If you are in a season when you know that you have kept your heart pure and are doing your level best and still face adversity, don't let Job's friends speak words of discouragement to you. I have lived long enough to know what Job knew. It rains on the just and the unjust. Bad things happen to good people. Great things happen to bad people. God is sovereign and you can't rebuke tragedy away and you can't earn one good thing from His hand. He is God. You are not.

I know a few of Job's friends. I have met them. They are still around after all these years. When they feel pain for you and can't fix something or figure it out – they find a scripture to place the blame somewhere; even if the last resort is you. Don't keep silent and rebuke them openly like Job did. Never come into agreement with them. Don't forget to also show mercy on them because they don't know any better. Pray for them like Job did and you will see even greater intimacy between you and your God.

Everyone's a Hypocrite!?

Everyone's a hypocrite. One time or another each person has been. *Merriam-Webster* defines a hypocrite this way: 1. A person who puts on a false appearance of virtue or religion. 2. A person who acts in contradiction to his or her stated beliefs or feelings.

No matter what god you serve or what religion (even if you lack one) you have been or are currently susceptible to hypocrisy. Definition number one is someone who purposely fakes their way through life and slaps on a tag of some form of goodness or darkness. I include darkness because I believe some people have a sense of God and pretend they don't. That would be hypocritical, wouldn't it? This definition number one, according to Merriam, is what polarizes most people to avoid religion altogether. Who would ever set out to live a lie?

Most of us, however, are prone to definition number two: acts in contradiction to his or her beliefs. Many people are fooled into thinking that they have never compromised their own beliefs.

I have also seen that being fearful of definition number one; a person who puts on a false appearance of religion... keeps people away from God. "WHY would I go to church and be a hypocrite if I KNOW I am going to drink alcohol when I want?" I have heard all the excuses. It just soothes the conscious knowing that one sin, hypocrisy, is one of which you refuse to be labeled. Better to be labeled a drunk. But the problem is this – you are still a hypocrite if you claim to be a Christian and pray but have your boundaries set at the cornerstone of hypocrisy - and that's where you won't cross the line in serving Him.

Deep down you know that one day the Lord might require you to stop drinking. Therefore, the human flesh tricks us and tells us not to even grace the door of our faith as to avoid being labeled.

If your fear of being a "hypocrite" is more dreadful to you than never meeting up with God in the first place, then I am here to set things straight. There are two forms of hypocrisy. Definition number two has touched all of us. None of us are exempt. So, everyone could technically be labeled a hypocrite.

My prayer is that if you have never "met up" with Jesus and pursued your real destiny in Him due to this issue of being phony...He has sought you out today to let you know that He is capable of handling what others may think of you. He knows that you will be hypocritical at times and wishes to rid you of your current state of it.

With or without Christ...we each contradict our beliefs; no matter what they are. Let me be among the first who isn't afraid to admit it.

I also find it curious that hypocrite has become a term relative to Christians. When was the last time you heard anyone call a Muslim or an atheist a hypocrite?

GOD OF THE BAD HOPS

A recent blurb in a Sports Illustrated Magazine said, "Things can turn out good - even bad hops." Caleb, my son, nudged me and grimaced when he pointed it out to me. We were sitting in the dentist's office and he had been using the magazine as a shield to hide his face. The night before he had taken a bad hop in practice and taken a blow from the baseball right to his front teeth. He thought it was really funny that he would have access to such a specific message as if sent to him directly - as encouragement. Was it a coincidence? We may never know.

I am reminded that despite what pain enters our lives we have a solid foundation in Christ. Any setbacks are manageable because we know God still has our best interest at heart. The mother in me can't yet find many good reasons for Caleb's palette folding like an accordion nor his mouth morphing into an ant-eater; but I know that it is temporary.

The Bible says that "...joy cometh in the morning." I am convinced that God loves my Son more than I do and that "this too shall pass." While we take time off from school and sports we will reflect on the bad hop with hopes that something good is just around the corner for him.

As Caleb said, "I guess this means I am on the D. L." (That's baseball talk for the "Disabled List.") I know that some of you may feel like you are in a perpetual state of being a bench warmer. Maybe you got cut from the team altogether. I want to encourage you; you have hope in Jesus and He can see you through to a victory. I am praying for you. I believe for you.

In the meantime all get- well cards and milkshakes that are being accepted at my home have caused Caleb to see just how many people love him. This is one good thing.

JESUS CALLED HER A DOG...

The cotton candy machine was fully engaged and the spools of pink and blue bundles were rising from the stainless dream maker. All the little kids ran up to my husband, Hugh, to watch as he was being sacrificially used to take the assault from the spun sugar. He described it as blown glass thrusting into his skin. I was busy selling the bagged candy clouds for the guests at the Fall Festival when I noticed the commotion increasing.

The kids discovered that if they stood close enough to Hugh that they could snatch a snack in the air as he made it. The wind lifted ribbons of sugar over the edge of the machine and they could stick out their tongue and capture a taste of heaven. Glee filled the air right alongside the drifting cotton candy. It wasn't long before adults caught wind of this event and put their tongues on display.

It reminded me of the good old days in North Alabama when a flurry of snow would come and we would try our hardest to catch a flake in mid-air ; we would feel as if we had somehow connected with something bigger than ourselves. Before I knew it puffs of pink and blue were all over the ground around us and folks were picking it up and popping it right into their mouths. The three second rule was into effect and no one had any shame.

This reminded me of a woman in Matthew chapter 15 who also had no shame. She asked Jesus to heal her daughter from an evil spirit. "Jesus refused, telling them, "I've got my hands full dealing with the lost sheep of Israel." Then the woman came back to Jesus, went to her knees, and begged. "Master, help me." He said, "It's not right to take bread out of the children's mouths and throw it to the DOGS." She was quick: "Your right, Master, but beggar dogs do get scraps from the Master's table." Jesus gave in. "Oh, woman, your faith is something else. What you want is what you get!" Right then her daughter became well.

There is so much healing power in the crumbs that fall from Jesus' table that you will never have a need to look elsewhere. If you or I feel unworthy to even sit at the table why don't we look down right where we are and see that leftovers are lying at our feet. You and I can pretend that we are not hungry for a Godly life and continue on in the pangs of starvation but we only cheat ourselves. I have decided that I will take God's doggy bag any day versus the life of entertaining and dining with evil spirits.

Those children who gathered to whisk away the goods are much wiser than the ones who purchased cotton candy from me that day. Let's take a lesson from them. All that God has in store for us is free for the taking. If we push our plates of pride aside we can taste and see that the Lord is good.

By the way … He said that He is preparing a table for us in the presence of our enemies. When I sit down to the feast of wholeness today I will be asking if cotton candy can be the dessert.

IF GOD WERE AMERICAN

There were 64 countries represented and the antici-
pation was as thick and as frustrating as a milkshake
when it gets stuck in a straw. This day... it mattered
that babies were crying (especially for the Somalian
lady in front of me). It was time to take the natural-
ization oath and no one needed the distractions. Every sound was being sifted in the room to make sure
that no one missed their name being called. There
was too much on the line. The American officers were
doing their best at pronunciation but each time those
babies howled it sent irritation throughout the atmo-
sphere.

Before we knew it a burly bald-headed guy was getting our attention. Using his best English he asked

my husband if he was going to take his test that day. He also began a negative dissertation about his Bosnian brother and cousin and how that they had failed miserably at their last attempts to become citizens. He had a few curse words laced into his story and spoke of the war that he had been dragged through as an eight year-old and constantly complained that he needed to go outside to smoke. But, he knew the moment he stepped out that they would call his name and he might miss his chance. He had been smoking since the age of eight and said that in his country if you are old enough to walk and "could drag the alcohol home," you could buy it. He announced how American rules are too strict and explained his many arrests since coming here at the age of sixteen.

It didn't take long for Hugh to begin to share his faith with this man but he wasn't having any of it. "If you don't smoke, don't drink, and don't chase hundreds of women, then what is your life?" He also said that God is too far away from someone like him and that even if we prayed for him that Mobile is too far away from Atlanta - where he called home. Our prayers wouldn't make it that far. The fellows from the Department of Homeland Security were just a few feet away and that was all he was interested in hearing about.

Just in that moment a Liberian man spoke up and said, "Man you have no excuse to keep making wrong decisions just because you had a rough life as a boy. You are now a man and can make the right decisions."

A tag team had occurred among men who were considered foreigners on this soil, yet, they shared a common bond of manhood and desired citizenship. I saw before my eyes three fantastically different skin tones on the men, incredibly different accents and vocal inflections, and very diverse backgrounds and experiences. But, the certificate they were all seeking seemed to level the playing field.

That was the case until the man from Thailand entered from stage left. It was shocking to all who watched. The herd of people gasped when he made his move and we all just knew that he would be denied his citizenship. The stamp would read on his paperwork, DENIED on the evidence of BEING ILLEGALLY RUDE. The she-male that was parading the applicants had a detailed and strict process for moving the lines along. When she was busy reprimanding the Vietnamese grandma the unassuming and brave Asian bolted and passed up everyone to make it to the front of the line.

Deep in my gut I laughed and thought…"hmmmm, he shall fit in very nicely here in America. He has already begun acting like one of us." Little did he know that he had to wait on every last human to enter the room before the ceremony could begin. And wait, we did. We waited. Then we waited some more. 9:30 am turned into 2:30 pm and we were still waiting. I laughed every time I caught a glimpse of this Thai man because his act of bravery only landed him a seat next to

Hugh. The man must have thought he could become American sooner if he took every advantage of the situation. I was tempted at one point to tattle on him to the beefy lady. I envisioned that her thigh-high, white Darth Vader boots would turn into the boots made for walking....for walking him right out of the building. But I watched anxiously instead to see if his skipping line afforded him any special privileges. It did not.

The same is true in our walk with the Lord. The blood of Christ levels the playing field. We are all foreigners here on the earth according to scripture and without the Certificate of Citizenship to Heaven (by being born again) we are illegal immigrants without a home. But once we take the "oath" by asking Jesus to save us and to enter into our lives - we sign over our rights to our own will and desires. We take on the Holy scriptures as our manual for our way of life. At that time all other potentates and authorities become null and void and our former citizenship is banished. No one is going to get there any other way. Jesus is the only way to the Father. One can climb any ladder built by human hands or even skip to the front of the line. God promises that it will only lead to the dead end of endless waiting for relief. There will be none. I can't imagine a place where the worm never dies and where those "babies never stop crying."

I pray that you will not be like the Bosnian man who rejected his own value from the loving God's perspective. I also pray you are not like the Thai man who thinks you can cheat or bypass God's laws and still get ahead. You may not get caught here but God promises that you won't reap any long-term benefits from it. By the way... they all became Americans on that day and now have every benefit that I have as a native American. No other country in the world has this opportunity. Likewise, no other God but Jesus can save us from the war-torn condition of our own hearts and let us live an abundant life. I hope your name is in the citizenship papers called the Lamb's Book of Life and inscribed with the blood of Christ. I also pray that your name will not be blotted out. Ever.

IF TYSON/HOLIFIED HAD BEEN IN THE GARDEN OF GETHSEMANE

The sound of the wind as it whipped past the torches' flame would've distracted me. The soldiers' weapons brilliant in it's light would have caused me to try to think of something else. But of course, I am not Malchus. But, if I had been him perhaps I would have known that this was my moment to "shine." He was, after all, the High Priest's right hand man; and they were headed to arrest, Jesus, the blasphemer-heretic. I remember a time when I was like Malchus. Full of myself and on a misinformed mission. I still struggle sometimes with the temptation.

I have had intentions of changing my world- my way. You and I know that this man must have been a beast; courageous with a razor-sharp mind to have been given special privileges to the most famous priest of his day. It may have been equivalent to being the Pope's bodyguard in our current times. We know this would be a noble job with many responsibilities. I believe that is why Malchus was the one to first lay his hands upon Jesus to seize Him. Everyone in the entourage knew the battle ranks. It had to be Malchus.

However, Malchus had met his match. He didn't know that Jesus also had a brave heart right hand man, named Peter. We all know about Peter's personality. He was the disciple that would jump ship to follow at a second's notice. He was the disciple that was rash and full of risk. He walked on water for God's sake - literally. This night he would be in for the confrontation of his life. When Malchus put his hands on his (Peter's) Lord, who he loved, he reacted in the same unrestrained way - he cut off Malchus' ear with his sword. The gloves were off. The bell never had a chance to ring. He didn't think twice and he didn't look back. In that instant of chaos I am sure that the sounds of the weapons, shields, and shouts rose to a climax. The armor bearers of two opposing forces had met on a head on collision. Who would come out on top? Who would wear the belt? The pinnacle ended as quickly as it had started. Neither showboat would get their romance with glory nor the championship. Not that day.

Jesus interrupted both of the hot-heads' plans. The Mike Tyson/Evander Holifield moment was over. He knelt down, picked up the bloody ear, leaned over to Malchus and worked a miracle for him. Jesus, touching the side of his head, reattached Malchus' ear. I believe to the shame of them both. Peter must have been humiliated that his leader had silently rebuked him with his compassionate actions. Malchus must have had his "Come to Jesus moment" right in front of his boss, the High Priest. I am sure we, like Malchus, can't argue when perfect love and mercy triumphs over judgment.

Malchus may have very well lived the rest of his days fulfilling his position as the High Priest's employee, but I bet each time he ran his fingers through his hair on that side of his face or cleaned his ears that the glimmer on the cheekbones of the innocent man who was put to death under his regime flashed before his face. Get into his head for a moment and try to understand the magnitude of what happened to him that night in the Garden of Gethsemane. He had been touched by the son of God and there was proof of it that he couldn't ignore. It was affixed to the side of his head- permanently.

You and I are not much different from Malchus, or Peter for that matter. In fact, it doesn't really matter which "side" we are on or what we are zealous about in this lifetime. There has been a moment when the Creator of the Universe has fixed consequences for us that we actually deserved to live with. I am not ashamed to say that this happens about daily in my life. Actually, it happens moment by moment, if I'm honest with myself. Likewise, I am sure that if you have been breathing any length of days, that the Lord has also allowed a very embarrassing moment that you never saw coming- a reprimand that cuts to the bone.

May you and I not be tempted to be red-faced when Jesus corrects our mistakes openly. May we also be gracious to receive the miracles openly, too. I bet Malchus wasn't ashamed that Jesus had worked a healing for him. Jesus is the same, yesterday, today, and forever. If you are a "Peter" or a "Malchus" in your circumstances today...it doesn't really matter. His love and healing is available to you. Now. Each second. Just receive it. Your life can never be the same once you have been touched by the Master's hands.

God's Smartphone

The three and four year-olds bowed their heads. One young lady prayed for the caterpillar she had caught that day, making a gesture about how its head went "that way" when she picked it up. I think she injured it and was trying to give the Lord an instant replay. Another pre-schooler from the the Wednesday night Bible class prayed for his toys. I could tell that I was to be silent and let each of them take their respective turns. Yet, another boy laced his fingers, tucked his chin deeper and said, "I don't have a Blackberry." That is all he said. The next one in the tiny blue chair next to him reeled off her thankfulness that she was now a big sister. I was amazed at the pureness of the prayers, but couldn't shake the announcement about being Blackberry deficient.

As the class progressed I pulled out the latest and greatest arts and crafts material to teach about the parable of the lost sheep. The truth is- and as is common- for three and four year-olds...they could have cared less. My shiny stickers couldn't keep their attention. They became increasingly bored with my Sign Language antics, my clowning, and my skills as a teacher. So I fell under the pressure. I defaulted. I slowly walked over to "the closet" and reached for a DVD. Shockingly, I now had their undivided attention. They began to reprimand each other to sit still and to be quiet, "SO WE CAN WATCH THE MOVIE!!!!!" Blissful squeals had erupted all over the room. It was a Bible DVD and they did pay attention. Their little bodies fell motionless under the power of the sound of the intro music ringing from the television speakers. Their little eyes glazed over, fixed, never blinking, gaping at the screen.

When I tell you they fell paralyzed under the influence of the disk, I mean they fell helplessly under its control. I sat their staring at them, as they stared at the box with sound and pictures. I felt a sincere sadness rush through my being. How heartbreaking it was that most of them were bored with words from humans; how sad that they were uninterested with materials to cut, paste, and color. No. They needed more exhilarating stimulation than that. They needed the almighty DVD!

It wasn't long before my sadness turned into conviction as I heard the Lord speak to my heart. He showed me a vision of the Me's and the You's as we sit behind our Smartphones and our social media with the same, blank, mindless expression. He told me, "I know how you're feeling. I feel the exact way about you. You have become more entertained with the things... instead of the Real Thing." I could do nothing in His presence but agree with Him and barely form the question of how it had come to be. He wasn't harsh with me and He didn't seem to be attention deficit and needy for my attention. It was just a mere observation that the Lord and I shared.

I determined that day to no longer be ashamed that my children are the only ones I know that don't have cell phones. I also became resolute to be more mindful of how I spend my time with things instead of ... the Only Real Thing. I hope your prayer is not like the one in my pre-school class. I hope that you DO have a Blackberry, a GPS system, Blue Ray, an I-Pod, or any other blessings that can come from the Lord. More importantly than that, I pray that you have ---the Lord of the blessings. He loves you and I even when we become bored with Him and His ordinary things.

Yard Sale Bandit?

I was forced to have a yard sale. My husband said he would not tolerate another day of holding on to so much junk, not to mention he said, "We could use the extra cash that it would bring." What he didn't know was that some of what he called junk wasn't junk at all. For instance, he was unaware that mingled into the pile were a few pieces of jewelry that I hadn't really broken in - but was planning to add into my rotation. So, I thought I would outsmart him by putting them into the sale at a much higher price point, secretly hoping they wouldn't sale, and then I could nonchalantly add them back into the storage. Nobody hurt. But, if they sold at the prices I put on them - it would really be a shocking blessing. He would be impressed.

Some demure southern belle showed up to the Yard Sale who loved the pieces of jewelry as much as I did. I kept my eye on her and the jewels. Oh, she played with them, rolled them over in her hand, caressing them, she even tried them on. In fact, she loved them so much she stuffed them confidently away into her bag and left. I was told by an on looking customer that after she paid me the $2.50 for another pair of cheap earrings that she saw her do it. She did it when I looked away. I was clueless. I didn't keep my eye on her because I thought she would really steal something from a garage sale. I wanted to see what would happen. But times must be harder than even I am aware.

I knew immediately what to do-I would pray for the thief but before I got to it the other customer exclaimed sarcastically, 'God is not gonna let her enjoy those pieces!!" So I responded; I prayed out loud for the Bandit, asking God to help her and to bless her... and the little ole lady, full of justice, concurred with an even louder, "Amen!!"

Well, after I had been deflated by the robbery and after Lady Justice left, I decided to pack it in for the day. Only one car actually pulled all the way into my driveway and it was the Bandit. Right where she had parked and gotten in and out of her car had been a little, green, dirty, make-up bag lying on the concrete. I was all alone and looked around. She had left a parting gift? OOPS. She must be new to the game of Bonnie and Clyde. I went over to the green bag, cautiously thinking it might come alive or something. But, my curiosity got the best of me. I unzipped it (looking inside with one eye open) and there was a wad of Cash, Greenbacks, Denero, the Benjamins. I immediately did some quick math in my head- it was almost the exact amount that the jewelry would have been... had she paid for it. I thought, WOW, you did a quick one here, Lord. In thankfulness to see that the Lord cared enough to show me He is in control...I went and pulled the necklace that the woman had also scoped out yet left behind. This time I put the necklace into the bag- her dirty, green makeup bag with cash in it.......and I waited. I was going to give her my "cloak when she had already taken my coat." Would she come back? Did she have the nerve? I was poised and ready to bless her, not only with her cash back, but another parting gift comprised of a match- ing necklace to set off the new ring and earrings that she had stolen. But, a week has passed and I haven't seen hide nor hair of her. I am beginning to doubt that I will.

Maybe you have had a Bandit or two to show up in your lifetime. Maybe things haven't come to life be- fore your very eyes like it did for me at my Yard Sale... YET. But, it can and I suggest that it will. Be on the lookout for God to make Himself known. He is very eager to show you His hand as it works on your behalf. When life sends you Bandits and they take precious things from you that you have worked hard for, look to God who is the Avenger. He never disappoints. Bless you today as you remember to keep your trust in Him - not being distracted by the Takers, Players, and Haters in this world. The Bible says, "Vengeance is mine, says the Lord, and I shall surely repay." Aren't you glad?

If God chose the car...

I recently took a spin in a friend's car and had quite a surprise in store. This friend admitted that she felt a bit "pretentious" driving it, and that she would rather stick to something a little more inconspicuous of opulence... like her other car. The "other car" happens to be a gleaming, pearl Cadillac Escalade. That statement alone was enough to make me giggle. So, giggling - we were off. We were on our way to lunch in the stunning Mercedes S550! As we pulled out of the driveway I thought I had touched some button because the seat was making movements all around me. Later, as we rounded the corner I felt a slight nudge from the side. "Am I losing my mind?", I thought. I knew I hadn't touched anything this time. Then it hit me. I am in a L-U-X-U-R-Y car. Of course, the seat, itself, was making the adjustments for me - to keep me comfortable during the "in-flight" highway drive aboard this car-craft!

Thefamilycar.com put it this way in it's review of the Mercedes S550:
"You see, when you are driving along a winding road at any kind of speed that may impart some side-to-side G-forces, you will feel the seat change shape as the side bolsters quickly inflate on the appropriate side to hold you in place. If there is minimal G-forces, you will hardly feel any movement, but toss the car into a turn and the bolsters will rapidly respond with additional force to counteract any unpleasant jostling. The computer receives signals from 13 sensors that monitor body movement and vehicle level and can make adjustments in thousandths of a second to counteract undesirable body movements before you ever feel them."

So what do you think this makes me think of....you guessed it. The Holy Spirit. He is always on the look out for turbulence and is running interference for us. Even when I am mishandling my life, He is cushioning my falls and giving me a safe place to land. If I round the corner of life too fast with my hasty decisions or making a fool of myself, once again, He is there to smooth out the course for me. If an enemy arises, known or unknown, and is out to do me harm...His sensors are on full alert.

I was vehemently reminded that day in the car that if a manufacturer caters to its customers with such high tech capabilities, what do you think the One who created their minds is able to do? I want to remind you today that the Holy Spirit, whether you can feel it or not, is bolstering you on every side. He is constantly protecting you from the winds of life that blow your way and is keeping you in your seat - safely.

You may be traveling a difficult path, you may have no cash, nor a clunker. Perhaps you can't even hitch a ride in this season of your life. Be encouraged. This too shall pass and there are great things in store for you as long as you allow the Father to be your chauffeur.

I pray for blessings for you today and that you may come to know the fullness of His riches, in Christ Jesus, our Lord.

Athlete's Feet

What's in a pair of shoes? Just ask the dude I just watched pay four grand for a pair of Albert Pujols cleats. Or, ask the young boy spotted in the aftermath of Hurricane Katrina. His family's home in Mobile, Alabama, was flooded and the rising waters washed away their belongings, obviously, including their shoes.

A partner of our ministry, we will call him Charlie, explains the situation to us: Driving around to assess the damage after the storm, he spots him-- a young boy outside his home in bewilderment (with no electricity) trying to take refuge in the front yard for a chance of feeling a cool breeze. Perhaps he was trying to escape the ninety-plus degree heat, the humidity, and the pain of what awaited him inside his home. A feeling of "What can I do to help him?" surges through Charlie's soul- and then he spots them... his feet; all wrapped up with newspapers and rubber bands twisted around his ankles. Charlie quickly pulls the vehicle over to the side of the road. He takes the sandals off of his own feet to give the boy. This is a moment that neither the boy, nor Charlie will ever forget. How could a child, so innocent, and precious in the sight of God, be using newspapers for shoes? This is normal in other countries but not here. Not in America.

The Bible says that "...All things work together for good to them that love God, to them who are called according to his purpose." (Romans 8:28) Charlie recounts this story to us only after we call him to ask him the shoe sizes of all of his family members. We needed the sizes so that we could send him brand new shoes that were donated to us for Hurricane relief. Charlie had taken in family that became dislocated due to the storm and we wanted to help him. Charlie says to us tearfully, "When I gave the boy the shoes off of my feet I wasn't looking for ANYTHING in return!" I submit to you today, when you do good to the least of these ...you are doing it unto Jesus, Himself, and He notices. We think He especially takes pleasure when you give- not expecting anything in return, according to Luke 6:35. Matthew 6:3 says, "When thou doest alms, let not thy left hand know what thy right hand doeth...or in Charlie's case - not knowing what your right foot is doing.

BRINGIN' HOME BLUE

Blue was a troublemaker. That dog was mean to passersby and had a reputation in the neighborhood as a menace. He would bark and growl at the smallest child and dare the biggest men to look his way. However, Blue was well loved by his master and she justified his behavior as "protecting his owners." Each time we visited we would try to develop a new strategy of how to get him under control.

I got an urgent phone call early one morning. Through many tears, Blue's owner explained how the night before, Blue didn't come home. I knew that meant trouble and offered my prayers and sympathy to the dog owner. Blue had finally met his match. Was he poisoned? Did he get bitten by a snake? All of these questions swirled in our heads. A search party was dispatched into the woods and they looked for hours on end.

As dusk fell and still no sign of Blue, Naomi and I hopped in the car, drove to the dog owner's neighborhood and began to call his name from the windows of the car. "Blue!, here boy. Blue. Blue." Boy did we feel foolish. All of the neighborhood knew who Blue was and a few of them looked at us in disgust. But, the tears of his owner compelled us to press on.

Once we arrived home I remember how swollen the face of Blue's master was from crying all day and I was moved with compassion. I asked God, aloud: "God, is it wrong to really keep believing you for something like this? Is this too small to bother you with?" You see, I am not the biggest animal lover in the world. I often think there are many more important issues to conquer. I struggle sometimes because animals are treated better than humans in some cases. Still, I questioned the Lord. "Would you work a miracle so that the broken heart of Blue's owner can be mended?" Troubled, I laid my head on the pillow.

The next thing I remember is the phone ringing at one o'clock in the morning. It was that same shaky voice saying, "Blue's home and he is banged up pretty bad. Thanks for your prayers." I hung up the phone and thanked God for His miracle. The next morning we drove to see him. Surprisingly, Blue was humbled now. No barking. No growling. Only blinking of his pretty blue eyes and wagging of his tail. He had road burns from head to toe. His front, left leg was raw, mangled, and double its normal size. He was headed to the vet for surgery.

Once again I asked the Lord, "What could've Blue been doing all those hours that we were looking for him? What suffering he must have been going through?" And oh yeah, Why did you bring him home, Lord? You know Blue is a rascal." Then I heard the Lord speak to me in His still, small voice. "Rascal? Rascal? So are you."

I remember a holy silence fell in my heart. Then He said, "I do the same thing with you - every single day. I call your name as you drag your mangled legs. In your own strength you cannot make it home. I just keep calling, just like you and Naomi did for Blue. I keep saying your name. Your spirit hears me and through the pain and suffering you keep heading my way."

It reminds me of how the father would go out each day and watch for his prodigal son to return. It didn't matter that he was a rascal, that he had squandered his inheritance, or that he was living a riotous lifestyle. The father continued to hope against hope. Today, your Heavenly Father is calling your name. He wants to bring you home...just like he did for Blue. He wants us to step out of the dark shadows and into the light of Heaven each and every day.

ABOUT THE AUTHOR

Jennifer Lopes is an ordained minister and Co-Founder of A More Excellent Way Ministries. She has a unique gift as a communicator and writer.

Professionally, Jennifer maintained dual national certification as an American Sign Language interpreter and owned an interpreting agency before being called into ministry full-time in 2005.

Jennifer's leadership and ability to disciple others has afforded her the opportunity to facilitate Bible studies for professional athletes' wives, to lead women's groups and speak at women's conferences and events.

Jennifer is an authority on the sanctity of human life, purity and youth leadership making her a national role model as an advocate for the unborn. She serves alongside her family in ministry and is a devoted wife and mother. She enjoys serving crisis pregnancy centers and seeing young people find their identity in Christ. She currently resides in Mobile, AL where she directs a national missions outreach. She can be reached at www.jenniferlopes.org.